Brian Jones

Printed and bound in Great Britain by MPG Books Ltd, Bodmin

Distributed in the US by Publishers Group West

Published by Sanctuary Publishing Limited, Sanctuary House, 45–53 Sinclair Road,
London W14 0NS, United Kingdom

www.sanctuarypublishing.com

Cover image: © Corbis

While the publishers have made every reasonable effort to trace the copyright owners
for any or all of the photographs in this book, there may be some omissions of
credits, for which we apologise.

ISBN: 1-86074-544-X

Brian Jones
Alan Clayson

Sanctuary

To all at Dawn's View

'BRIAN, YOU'RE SO ESOTERIC!!!'

– placard hoisted by a member of the audience when
The Rolling Stones appeared at the Cobo Hall, Detroit,
Michigan on 26 November 1965

Contents

About The Author

Born in Dover, England, in 1951, Alan Clayson lives near Henley-on-Thames with his wife, Inese, and sons, Jack and Harry. His portrayal in the *Western Morning News* as 'the AJP Taylor of the pop world' is supported by *Q*'s 'his knowledge of the period is unparalleled and he's always unerringly accurate'. He has written many books on music, including best-sellers *Backbeat* (subject of a major film) and *The Yardbirds*, as well as for journals as diverse as *The Guardian, Record Collector, Mojo, The Times, Mediaeval World, Eastern Eye, Folk Roots, Guitar, Hello!, The Independent, Ugly Things* and, as a teenager, the notorious *Schoolkids' Oz*. He has also performed and lectured on both sides of the Atlantic, as well as broadcasted on national TV and radio.

From 1975 to 1985 he led the legendary group Clayson And The Argonauts and was thrust to 'a premier position on rock's Lunatic Fringe' (*Melody Maker*). As shown by the formation of a US fan club – dating from a 1992 *soirée* in Chicago – Alan Clayson's following has continued to grow, as has demand for his talents as a record producer and the number of cover versions of his compositions by such diverse acts as Dave Berry – in whose Cruisers he played keyboards in the mid-1980s – and New Age outfit Stairway. He has also worked with The Portsmouth Sinfonia, Wreckless Eric, Twinkle, The Yardbirds, The Pretty Things and the late Screaming Lord Sutch, among others. While his stage act defies succinct description, he is spearheading an English form of *chanson*. Moreover, his latest album, *Soirée*, may stand as his artistic apotheosis, were it not for the promise of surprises yet to come.

Further information is obtainable from www.alanclayson.com

Prologue
Foundation Stone

'Well, he was different over the years as he disintegrated. He ended up the kind of guy that you dread he'd come on the phone – because you knew it was trouble. He was really in a lot of pain – but in the early days, he was all right.'

– John Lennon[1]

While he wasn't someone you'd trust with either your heart or your cheque book, Brian Jones was the foundation stone of the group that, to the same arguable degree as The Beatles, soundtracked the Swinging Sixties. Moreover, if Mick Jagger was the mind, Keith Richards the heart and Bill Wyman and Charlie Watts the flesh and blood, the charismatic Jones – androgyny with underlying dread – was surely the soul of The Rolling Stones. He was also their James Dean, their Jet Harris, their Pete Best, their Ace Kefford, their Syd Barrett, their Sid Vicious.

He satisfies any requirement of a doomed rock hero: a loveless upbringing, bohemian wanderings, drug busts, neurotic self-absorption, aspirations to bridge a gap between lowbrow pop and higher artistic expression, a visual image that remains modern – and, to round it off, the 'beautiful sadness' of an early grave. Furthermore, Jones held for a long while some sort of British record as the pop star with the most number of known illegitimate offspring. Yet, despite the unquiet nature of his 27 years, Brian clung onto his good looks – just – retaining a boy's face, albeit one with a lot of miles in the eyes.

His was, therefore, a triumphant and tragic life in which he both glided high on pop's strongest winds and swam shoreless seas of despair. He has since moved into an orbit separate from that of the Stones. This has so strong a definition that a forthcoming biopic, *The Wicked World Of Brian Jones*, threatens to be *the* British movie of 2005, and an annual memorial event in Brian's home town of Cheltenham draws multitudes of pilgrims.

After drifting from pillar to post, from group to unsatisfactory group since his schooldays, the talented and musically adventurous Brian's musical career left the runway in 1962 when he formed The Rolling Stones, who, to his apparent chagrin, began moving away from their blues core during an accelerating run of hit singles written by Jagger and Richards. Though their abilities brought the group continued success, and may have saved Jones from a more mundane existence, his thwarted ambition as a composer deserves sympathy.

As he lost his grip on both the Stones and non-professional realities, Brian wanted to, but couldn't, rewind to 1962, when everything was possible. He wanted to, but couldn't, brush aside all the millennia that had passed since, like so many matchsticks. Once the group's livest wire, Jones was reduced to a pitiful isolate, shrouded in melancholy and paranoia, the twinkle vanished from his eye. His exit weeks before his death in 1969 did not, therefore, bring the Stones to their knees, as it might have done had he left six years earlier.

The posthumous legend continues to be nourished by half-truths, tidy-minded media fiction – and no less than six previous books about Jones, though none could be described as 'definitive'.

In this account, care has been taken to address the myriad social, cultural, economic, environmental and further factors that polarise and prejudice what is generally understood about Brian Jones already, and the new and rediscovered evidence and information that recent research has brought to light. Often pop biography – and that's all this is – has tended to shy away from these areas – even though they form a more tangible basis for investigation than treating flippant public remarks by the subject as gospel.

Those who devote themselves to collating facts about The Rolling Stones may pounce on mistakes and omissions while scrutinising this work. All I can say to them is that it's as accurate as it can be after the synthesis of personal memories and interviews with some of the key *dramatis personae* – not to mention filing cabinet drawers labelled 'Brian Jones', and exercise books full of doctor's prescription-like scribble drawn from press archives – some of them quite obscure.

Please put your hands together for Iain MacGregor, Laura Brudenell, Chris Harvey, Nikky Twyman, Claire Musters and the rest of the team at Sanctuary, who went far beyond the call of duty from this biography's sluggish genesis to its final publication.

I am also very grateful to Pat Andrews, Dave Berry, Mike Cooper, Don Craine, Keith Grant-Evans, Richard Hattrell, Mick M Jones, Phil May, Jim McCarty, Tom McGuiness, Brian Poole, Dick Taylor and Twinkle for their pragmatism, clear insight and intelligent argument.

Thanks are in order, too, for Jane Allen, Robin Brooks and Verity Herrington of the *Gloucestershire Echo,* as well as Brian Auger, Mick Avory, Jayne Down (of Cheltenham Reference Library), Jonathan Meades, Sally Pillinger, Roger Winslet and, especially, Trevor Hobley and John MacGillivray of The Brian Jones Fan Club.

Whether they were aware of providing assistance or not, let's also have a round of applause for these musicians: Roger Barnes, Alan Barwise, Cliff Bennett, the late Lonnie Donegan, Chris Gore, 'Wreckless' Eric Goulden, Brian Hinton, Robb Johnston, Garry Jones, Barb Jungr, Graham Larkbey, the late Noel Redding, Mike and Anja Stax, the late Lord David Sutch, John Townsend and Paul Tucker.

It may be obvious to the reader that I have received much information from sources that prefer not to be mentioned. Nevertheless, I wish to thank them – as well as B and T Typewriters, Bemish Business Machines, Stuart and Kathryn Booth, Peter Doggett, Ian Drummond, Katy Foster-Moore, Michael Heatley, Dave Humphries, Rob Johnstone, Allan Jones, Sarah Jones, Spencer Leigh, Doug Little, Elisabeth McCrae, Stefan Mlynek, Russell Newmark, Mike Ober, Mike Robinson, Mark Stokes, Stuart Stokes, Anna Taylor, Michael Towers, Warren Walters, Gina Way and Ted Woodings, and also Inese, Jack and Harry Clayson, for letting me get on with it – plus a special nod to Kevin Delaney.

Alan Clayson
October 2003

1 Along Came Jones

'He was a real idiot, Brian. He set out to be a rebel and to upset
people. He felt it was a thing he had to do. It was pointless because,
really, he was a quite a nice guy, and his parents were nice people.'
— *Ian Stewart*[1]

It was heralded with an extensive poster campaign, press advertisements
and extensive word of mouth. A show on the capacious bandstand of a
public park, it promised 27 bands plus a pageant of supplementary
entertainment. A calculated risk about the weather meant the audience
would be open to the sky but, even at dawn, the day was promising to
be a scorcher, and a buzzing multitude of thousands was already sprawled
across the greensward, many having arrived by train the previous evening.
Estimates varied but, if exaggerated, it was certainly one of the largest
assemblies for any musical event ever accommodated by the locality. The
tribes would depart afterwards, having participated, however passively,
in the proverbial 'something to tell your grandchildren about'.

The crowd's morning vigil was measured in expeditions for tepid
drinks – and, unless you had an iron bladder, concealing bushes en route
were not ignored. The gathering tension was also punctuated by
announcements from a master of ceremonies with a sad gaucho moustache,
transmitting information about lost youngsters and the forthcoming
programme as well as pleas to consider the environment by not leaving
litter or climbing surrounding trees for a better view.

Could we be at a San Francisco 'Be In', circa late 1966? Waiting in
Hyde Park for The Rolling Stones? Castle Donington? Glastonbury?
Reading? Any major outdoor pop extravaganza since 1966? Actually, it's

the Grand Brass and Silver Band Contest, held in southeast Gloucestershire in Cheltenham's Pittville Park on 14 July 1868 where, though nine of the expected outfits declined to play, those that did mount the stage blared out a test piece called 'Venetian Waltz' plus one item of their own choice. Craning distant necks, and commanding attentive silences and considered ovations, The Worcester County Lunatic Asylum Band – selected from staff not patients – carried off the £16 ($27) first prize with entrants from Gloucester, Stroud and faraway Abertillery amongst runners-up. The greatest day anyone could ever remember concluded with fireworks 'prepared by Mr Grundy', and – as was proper – the massed 400 or so performers blasting up 'Rule Britannia' and the national anthem.

While such tournaments took place in Gloucestershire as early as the Industrial Revolution, the shire forged further opportunities for musical expression beyond trumping a euphonium in the Remembrance Day procession. The most famous musician Cheltenham ever produced, for instance, was to pen 'very catholic, but I hate brass bands' when filling in the 'Tastes in music' section of the *New Musical Express*'s 'Life-lines' questionnaire late in 1964.[2]

While Tony Sheridan (the vocalist The Beatles backed in 1961 when they began their commercial discography) and Mick Farren (leader of The Social Deviants, mainstays of Britain's 'alternative' circuit of one-nighters in the late 1960s) are connected by simple accident of birth, Brian Jones will be eternally, if reluctantly, Cheltenham's as The Beatles will be Liverpool's. Indeed, there are middle-aged folk who boast still of having sat next to Brian at infant school, sang in the same church choir or danced with a man who danced with a girl who danced with him at St Luke's Hall along Bath Road. The fellow who'd cadged a cigarette off you there – and Brian, they'd chuckle, was always one of nature's takers – had been the cynosure of unseen millions of eyes on the very first edition of *Top Of The Pops* on New Year's Day 1964.

Yet once Brian Jones had been, on the surface, an expressionless youth mooching along the pavement, and it had been impossible to deduce that, within his shell, he was an epitome of JB Priestley's assertion in his 1956 critique of Colin Wilson's *The Outsider,* 'that butchers cutting off chops may be touched by intimations of immortality, that the grocer, even as he hesitates over the sugar, may yet see the world in a grain of sand'. There'd been nothing to suggest that, like his immediate forebears, Brian too would not live a relatively uneventful life, even dwelling until the grave in the town that vied with Cirencester and Gloucester as stone-built 'capital' of the Cotswolds.

Cheltenham was remote enough, even after World War II, for the distance to the metropolis to be measured in years rather than kilometres. Bigoted Londoners still assumed that the further towards the Atlantic or Irish Sea you travelled, the more yokel-like the natives. Yet Cheltenham had thrived in its isolation and built-in resilience as an agricultural centre from the pre-Christian era, and as a Roman settlement, exemplified today by period pavements uncovered for public scrutiny then buried again to preserve against decay.

After the discovery of the medicinal properties of its waters, Cheltenham became a decidedly non-bumpkin spa in 1719 – and 'the most complete Regency town in England', according to the borough council's tourist guide book. Even in the 1950s, the River Chelt – a tributary of the Severn from Bristol – was a-swarm with coarse fish, but to most Britons the town remained just another point on the route between London and South Wales. To train travellers passing through, it seemed no different from any other town of sufficient inhabitants to warrant a railway station by the mid-19th century.

After the Great War, the names over the shops continued to change, but hikers still breasted the surrounding wolds where sheep nibbled on grassy old battlegrounds. Some open country remained just so – such as that within the estate of the aristocratic Mitfords, whose ancestral home, Swinbrook, stood near one of the outlying hamlets. Elsewhere, however, arcadian meadows were about to be buried beneath an urban overspill sprawl of residential hinterland of raw red brick, built by the book amidst small-time light industry, tangles of shopping precincts, arteries of droning traffic, rows of lock-up garages and industrial estates with their engineering, electronics, chemical and printing works.

Yet conservatism and long residency in Cheltenham remained prerequisites of entry into polite society, which contained broods connected either to old money or an officer class that, after a life of service to the Empire – particularly in India – had retired there with memoirs to think about writing, mounted heads of wild animals they'd shot and framed and yellowing photographs of themselves wearing pith helmets.

Along genteel Hatherley Road, geometrically patterned linoleum in the kitchen was among few hints of domestic personality in Ravenswood, a semi-detached that was, recalled Pat Andrews, one of Brian's first 'serious' girlfriends, 'modern, if quite spartan furniture-wise'. It was the Jones family's second home in Cheltenham, and it was there that Brian, still in nappies, had caught and held the sounds of Welsh as well as English.

Wales was close enough for Brian, as a round-eyed toddler, to have watched the RAF's diamond formations zooming towards the Luftwaffe's bombardment of the docks in both Newport and Bristol – facing each other across the Severn – where the horizon glowed with tonne upon booming tonne of death and destruction. Moreover, on 28 February 1942 – a cold but dry day during a year of meteorological extremes – he'd entered the world as Lewis Brian Hopkin-Jones, embracing the two most common surnames in the principality.

'One of his grandfathers was a schoolmaster in Wales,' explained Pat Andrews, adding that 'the family background was "Chapel", and enjoying yourself in any way played no part in their lives. You were born, you went to school, you made sure you got good marks, you found yourself a good profession, you got married, you had children – and that was it. There was no time in between for any fun.'

Outwardly, however, Mr and Mrs Jones were 'nice people', conventionally conscientious rather than doting parents who endeavoured to instil into their son what ought to be admired about quiet dignity and achievement by effort. This they did during a period when it was common for offspring to be berated in harsh and penetrating tones in the most public places. These days, it would be called either 'tough love' or 'child abuse'. Whatever it was, it wasn't very effective, and its perpetrators earned the adolescent Brian's scorn rather than filial devotion – though he would remain very concerned about parental disapproval even when ostensibly escaped from their clutches.

Home, therefore, was a place where Brian and sister Barbara, four years younger, kept their emotions in check, and where the good opinion of peers mattered more to Lewis and Louise than their children's happiness. Their only other child, Pamela, had died of leukaemia at the age of two.

'His mother told Brian that Pamela had been sent away for being naughty,' averred Pat Andrews, 'and he may have formed the impression then that it wasn't healthy to become too attached to anyone – because they'd leave you. His parents' behaviour wasn't intentionally cruel, but it was to do with the attitude then: that you had to be cruel to be kind – especially towards boys. Brian really suffered from this – particularly as he wasn't able to let his artistic nature surface, though, when he moved out, he painted a beautiful mosaic on the wall of his flat. His father wanted him to be an optician, a solicitor, an architect…something with a solidly professional veneer to it – though he could have just about handled it if Brian had wanted to be a classical musician.'

We would like the impossible: videos of scenes that busied the rooms of Ravenswood or to sample with Brian's own sensory organs how a particular glance, word or gesture from his mother would cow him, even as a young adult. In every family, there is always territory forbidden and inexplicable to outsiders, but it is probable that Brian suffered exultant application of corporal punishment as a boy, and was also subjected to rearing methods intended to force him not to feel bitterness or anger towards Mum and Dad, even when those feelings might be entirely justified.

All children are born in love with their parents. There is no God but Mummy, and Daddy is the prophet of Mummy. However, when Mummy and Daddy resort to hurting you, saying things, lying, the world stops making sense.

'Brian's baby picture is quite startling,' observed mid-1960s pop star Marianne Faithfull, 'A jowly, miserable child is looking up at you with exactly that expression of helpless victimisation he gave off in the last year of his life.'[3]

With his face scrubbed and his blond hair combed until his entire scalp was sore, Brian trudged along as the family paraded to and from divine worship at 900-year-old St Mary's Parish Church. Once there, Mum, Dad and Barbara took their seats in their usual high-backed pew while Brian went round to the vestry, where cassock, ruff and surplice were to cover the detested and sober suit that, when he began wearing spectacles and was old enough for long trousers, made him look like a miniature version of his father. As a matter of course, he had been obliged to join other boys who cantillated every Sunday and, when required, at weddings and in St Cecilia's Day oratorios. As he rose through the ranks, he'd be privileged sometimes to bear the processional cross as priest and choir filed in and out. He also doused the altar candles after the General Confession during Matins.

Yet the holy sounds he sang were slightly unintelligible (if occasionally extraordinary) at 9, and over-familiar and rote-learned by 13. As it is with every intelligent teenager, he began to question the motives of adult communicants. Were the rafter-raising votes of confidence and thanks to the Lord once a week to assuage His inferiority complex, to quench His restless thirst for applause or a stockpiling of spiritual ammunition for the defence when the worshippers' cases came up on Judgment Day?

He soon absorbed the habits of those choristers of the same kidney. Mostly, they were tiny, covert, cat's-cradling rebellions, but the story goes that, for an involuntary giggle during a sermon, Brian was subjected to an explosive churchyard tongue-lashing by Mrs Jones – which included a promise that he'd be 'sent to bed with the light off as soon as you get home' – so that sin rebuked by a godly woman would be witnessed by the others filing out after evensong.

From then on, at several points during each of the three services he endured every Sunday, Brian would direct as sincere a smile as he could muster at his mother in the congregation, in order to gauge the mood, relaxing only if the smile was returned as he sang into the tedium of enough churchgoing to last a lifetime.

Later, Brian would profess to be an atheist, but no one was sure whether to believe him because, for all his brashness, it's likely that at least a dark and lonely corner of his psyche remained superstitiously terrified of eternal punishment for sin. Another legacy of his boyhood were lengthening bouts of depression and lifelong nervous disorders that either triggered or were aggravated by chronic asthma. Certainly, it drove out both a capacity for uninhibited joy and any pleasant recollections of life in a dysfunctional home where, through lace curtains, he'd glower and wonder if this was all there was.

In reciprocation, Lewis, relaxing over an after-dinner crossword in plain cardigan and baggy trousers, couldn't understand what his son found so loathsome about a decent life in a country town where the only times a true gentleman's name appeared in the *Gloucestershire Echo* was on the occasion of his marriage and when he shuffled off this mortal coil.

A lot of Brian's parents lived on in him, but a positive side of the soul-murdering persecution from so-called loved ones was his liberalism during those brief periods when, before the novelty wore off, he was actively involved in his own children's upbringing after he'd understood that there might be openings other than in secure but – to Brian – dull jobs like Dad's at Dowty and Co aeronautical engineering works, with Eldorado a bonus in your pay packet. Perish the thought, but you might be better off as the scion of some unrespectable coalman or bus conductor who didn't frown should you ask to go to the cinema on the Sabbath and wouldn't threaten to disinherit you if you dared to come downstairs in an American tie.

GIs on passes had burst upon the fun palaces of Cheltenham in garb in which only blacks, London spivs and the boldest homosexuals would be seen dead – padded shoulders on double-breasted suits with half-belts at the back, 'spear-point' shirt collars, two-tone shoes and those contentious hand-painted ties with American Indians or baseball players on them. Sartorial visions, they would acknowledge bemused or envious stares with waves of fat wands of cigars. At one stage during World War II, it was reckoned that North Americans stationed in the town had outnumbered the British residents.

Though few lights had showed along the tree-lined Promenade at night, it was jammed with US army vehicles. Traffic was as heavy up and down stairs in at least two prominent hotels that had become part-brothel, part-casino, and where you'd be scrutinised through a spyhole and refused access if you were less than a lieutenant.

Lower ranks whooped it up in the noise and crush of those pubs where prostitutes were welcome, mingling with parochial roughnecks until representatives from Gloucester of the most fearsome if narcissistic of post-war youth cults descended on Cheltenham one evening in the pre-rock 'n' roll 1950s. Resplendent in their seedy-flash finery and quiffed glaciers of brilliantine, the Teddy Boys were wielding flick knives and bicycle chains. They had some grievance against the US visitors, and the expedition climaxed with the killing of a GI in the bus station toilets. One outcome of this incident was that the whole town was declared off limits to North American servicemen.

The US presence also marked the genesis of Cheltenham's participation in Britain's attempts to get to grips with jazz, a form detested by Lewis Jones in his office as sometime organist at St Mary's, as it was by Louise, a piano teacher, even if Stravinsky had been, in 1913, sincerely loud in his praise of jazz, thus elevating it from a slang expression to describe the improvised extrapolations prevalent in negro dance music.

Regardless of who was present, Mr or Mrs Jones would switch off the wireless if it was broadcasting not only jazz, but also whatever else they had lumped derisively together as 'swing' – because it epitomised the depraved cacophony that was the distinguishing feature of the modern music that was subverting all that was good and true. Hitler had had his faults, but pouring contempt on that rubbish hadn't been among them.

'To Brian's parents, jazz was black music, played in speakeasies,' elucidated Pat Andrews, 'anything to do with it was connected with drugs and sex. Brian had problems listening or playing any sort of music there. It wasn't to be too loud. He'd rarely practise at home, apart from piano which his mother taught him, and clarinet. He played piano in a duet on a school open day, and his father was very proud of Brian's rendition of Weber's *Clarinet Concerto*.'

It was beyond them to be too demonstrative about it, but his parents were delighted at their first-born's inherited musical strengths, and his willingness from earliest youth to try, try again as he sweated over Bach, Chopin and further prescribed exercises that revealed to him that music was a science as much as an art. Brian was also self-contained enough to disassociate it from the drudgery, albeit with Pat Andrews' qualification 'give Brian half an hour, and he could get something recognisable from any musical instrument, but the chase was better than the catch. Once he'd mastered the thing, he'd get tired and move onto something else.'

In a cultural atmosphere of diminished fifths and Brahms' *German Requiem* as well as the general oppressive *ennui* of Ravenswood and the ebbing Regency calm of his home town, Brian had been sheltered as far as possible from bohemianism as the country paid for its victory, and the West Country continued to be pictured in metropolitan breakfast rooms as a corner of the map where nothing much was guaranteed to happen, year in, year out.

Morris Minor 'woodies', bulbous Ford Populars, Ford Anglia delivery vans with the grocer's name on the side-panelling and the odd Morris 100 police car could park with ease and without restriction along the High Street where the number 6 bus began and ended its ding-dinging, stop-start commute to Warden Hill, and the offices of the *Gloucestershire Echo* then cooked up its weekly diet of whist drives, winter farrowing, the Operatic Society's production of *Merrie England*, gypsies camped illegally on a disused army camp, the Rotary Club's 'celebrity' football match, horse-racing results and the more intriguing lots at forthcoming house auctions.

This was spiced with less run-of-the-mill news such as Diana Dors, Britain's 'answer' to Marilyn Monroe, opening a new electrical wholesaler's along the High Street; Cotswold peer Lord Wogan-Phillips outing himself as the first Communist member of the House of Lords and the rebuilding of the council offices after a fire in 1960 – but, as it was in most other English provincial towns, the 1950s didn't really end in Cheltenham until about 1966, and bored adolescents with hormones raging wondered what to do until bedtime just as they had since archers had trained on the green prior to setting off for Agincourt. All the alleged excesses of a wider world belonged to speculation while sharing a communal filter-tip behind school bicycle sheds, and rare sightings of the odd student emerging from the art college, carrying a huge painting of a nude, and accompanied by a female who was identifiable as its subject.

Brian Jones's formal education had started at fee-paying Dean Close Primary School, a middle-class version of Cheltenham Gentlemen's

College, a public (ie private) school that was to be the location for *If*, the 1968 film about a bloody rebellion against the staff and governors by a coterie of schoolboys.

At Dean Close, Brian sailed through the 11-plus in 1953, and thus gained a place at the grammar school that was between the bus depot and the brewery, with the art college situated on its top two floors. For Lewis and Louise, it was as desirable a social coup as an academic one for Brian to be seen in the grammar's black-and-white-striped blazer and cap rather than the uniform – if there was such a thing – of one of Cheltenham's secondary moderns, where 'failures' went before the advent of the fairer 'education for all' comprehensive system allowed you (theoretically) to follow what best suited your abilities and inclinations as they evolved.

Whether he'd become famous in later life or not, Brian Jones would have been remembered as more than a name on a register at the grammar. As a first-former, all eyes and teeth, in the top academic stream, he settled down almost eagerly to classwork, but, as it was with boring, boring church, he wearied of the draconian affectations and futile rigmarole. Two terms might have transformed another of the same mind into a capable but uninvolved student, unblinking in the monotony of, say, the geography master's chalky exposition of Belgium's inner waterways, but Brian's disinterest could not remain passive, and the more faint-hearted teachers discovered a feeling of relief whenever he was absent.

'Somewhere along the line, he decided he was going to be a full-time professional rebel,' sighed Keith Richards, 'and it didn't really suit him – so that when he wanted to be obnoxious, he had to really make an effort, and, having made the effort, he would be really obnoxious.'[4]

By the end of his second year at the grammar, Brian Jones was a known nuisance. Already, he had become a sharer of smutty stories and magazines of female lingerie and, despite his respiratory maladies, was a member of a caste that had graduated from the innocence of tooth-rotting Spangles to the lung-corroding evil of cigarettes.

More overt offences began with insulting 'politeness' to teachers, red-herring time-wasting tactics in class and dumb insolence when directed to spit a sweet into the litter bin during lessons. Then came an appearance behind an inkwelled desk in football boots – 'more comfortable,' he argued – rather than the regulation black 'bombhead' shoes; instigating a widespread and hastily suppressed practice of bottled beer instead of the third-pints of lukewarm milk then provided at morning break, courtesy of the Welfare State – and earning a week's suspension for ringleading a mutiny against the prefects. Far from being homicidally *If*-like, this prank was as ineffectual and as banal as the others when, for all the school's cradling of Cheltenham's intellectual elite, might was right in the face of Brian's ability to nutshell and, smoothly and logically, contradict the most complex arguments for toeing the line at school. Yet it diverted attention from the fact that Brian was as craven a physical coward as Flashman in *Tom Brown's Schooldays*. If slightly below middle height like his father, he was broad-shouldered and had a soft husk of a voice that, even with its noticeable lisp, could sound menacing. At school and beyond, Brian could exert a vice-like grip on his allies in delinquency, some of whom weren't so much friends as disciples whom he could persuade to do almost anything. Among them would be the type of specimen that, ostensibly unbothered and faithful, might be lured into some shaming *faux pas*, sent on a fool's errand and driven to near-suicide with mind games.

Some of Brian's 'victims', however, either weaned themselves off him or started to snap back. A few went so far as to put up their fists and look fierce, noting how swiftly their antagonist would back down. They'd ascertained that, beneath the bravado, Brian was, psychologically, a bit of a 'weed'. This was corroborated by the fear in his grey-green eyes when summoned to be confronted with his infamy in headmaster Dr Arthur Bell's study, and the latter's informed obituary for Brian in the school magazine in autumn 1969: 'Brian Jones seemed to be essentially a sensitive and vulnerable boy, not at all cut out for the rough-and-tumble of the commercial world.'

Dr Bell agreed, too, that 'he always seemed quite clever, and he did in fact do quite well – though nothing like as well as he might have done had he been attracted to an academic career'. Whatever the stomach-knotting repercussions of the turmoil he caused, and however profound his apparent indifference to logarithms and the Diet of Worms, Brian answered barked questions correctly and succinctly without seeming to awake from a daydream, and didn't lose a knack for passing examinations, even those most important ones held during summer when, shirt-sleeved in the heat, and with pen sliding in sweaty palm, his asthma allied with hay fever.

On the raw statistics of results, Brian was a credit to his parents, and a 'nice little boy' to outsiders. In denial, his mother might recall a loving relationship with her fallen angel, lots of cuddles, full of fun, until he became impossible to live with, what with the increasing trouble about his choice of friends of either sex; his late hours and his insolence; those crude drainpipe jeans and other of the more ridiculous clothes he'd got past her quality control, and the way he treated other members of the family. She and Lewis would have to all but disown him after the scandal that caused him to leave the grammar school under the darkest cloud possible.

2 Someone Else's Baby

'From when Brian was about fifteen, his mother and father felt he was a bad influence on his sister, so he wasn't really allowed to have much to do with her.'

– Pat Andrews

By the mid-1950s, you'd come across the most unlikely brass bandsmen buying a ticket automatically for not only a Cheltenham International Festival of Music event – at the racecourse, say, or at Berkeley Castle or Pittville Pump Room – but a Town Hall jazz concert, and being able to discuss with authority such erudite subjects as 'small-band Ellingtonia' or dropping buzz words like 'Monk', 'Miles Davis', 'Getz' and 'Brubeck' into conversations.

Gloucestershire was to be well represented with Dixieland units, but even during the traditional jazz – 'trad' – boom in the early 1960s, the county produced few musicians from a jazz background of comparable national renown to bowler-hatted Bristol clarinettist Acker Bilk, trumpeter Kenny Ball from Ilford, Glaswegian trombonist George Chisholm with his comedy routines on BBC television's *Black And White Minstrel Show* or even cornetist Ken Colyer, who, within London's Crane River Jazz Band, formed, arguably, the first British skiffle group in 1949 as an intermission from the interweaving of the front-line horns – though, two years later, The Washboard Wonders took up one side of Chris Barber's New Orleans Jazz Band's first extended-play (EP) disc.

The most famous – if that is the word – Cheltenham jazzer was Tony Mann. His prodigious hand-and-foot coordination earned him a post in the all-purpose combo at London's Ronnie Scott's, storm centre of

UK jazz, serving Sonny Rollins, Stan Getz, Cannonball Adderley and other visiting North Americans.

Dotted bebop crochets on Tony's ride cymbal – *ching-a-ching-ching* – had no place in rock 'n' roll, but other drummers were socking a crude but powerful off-beat behind local pop singers. However, as there'd be no Cheltenham Acker Bilk, so there'd be no 'answers' to would-be UK Elvis Presleys such as Tommy Steele, Cliff Richard, Marty Wilde and Billy Fury or even also-rans like Terry Dene, Dickie Pride or Vince Eager.

So parochial was provincial pop that there seemed to be no halfway between obscurity and the Big Time. Certainly, Gloucestershire spawned a paltry litter of hit parade contenders of even Eager-sized renown in the principal domain of groups that began during the late 1950's skiffle craze – coffee bars and youth clubs that convened mostly in musty Victorian monstrosities where soft drinks, with-it vicars and a wholesome, self-improving reek were the norm.

Yet the music heard within their walls – the likes of 'Midnight Special', 'Rock Island Line', 'This Little Light Of Mine', 'How Long Blues' and sweetly sinister 'Careless Love' – was the same in essence, but the setting was in another dimension to the rent parties, speakeasies and rowdy Dust Bowl jug bands of the US Depression when Ken Colyer's seaman brother Bill spotted one such outfit working in Chicago, Dan Burley's Skiffle Boys, featuring a black singing guitarist called Brownie McGhee.

Ken's Crane River splinter group and The Washboard Wonders approximated this for British audiences. The latter consisted of Beryl Bryden on washboard and Chris Barber himself on double bass accompanying guitarist and banjoist Lonnie Donegan's brace of blues-tinged North American folk songs. It became the highlight of the show.

'This newly awakened interest in the true Negro "race" music which Chris and Lonnie have been fostering for some years, opens up a whole new field of traditional jazz,' read the sleevenotes to the Barber outfit's *New Orleans Joys* in 1954.[1] From this 10in LP, Donegan's 'Rock Island Line' was issued eventually as a single, spending months in the domestic Top 20 and prompting Lonnie to strike out alone. Further hits followed and, ennobled as 'King of Skiffle', Lonnie bossed the form during its 1957 prime, delving deeply into its hillbilly as much as its blues bedrock.

When skiffle started losing its flavour on the bedpost overnight, the more 'sophisticated' of its practitioners that hadn't fallen by the wayside were to switch to trad, what with 'The story of Folk Song with a Jazz beat' being the subtitle of clergyman Brian Bird's *Skiffle*,[2] a 1958 study regarded as the style's Bible and *Yellow Pages*.

According to the sleeve notes to a 1958 EP entitled *Chris Barber In Concert Volume Three* trad jazz was 'gay and carefree music'[3] – on paper, the antithesis of blues. Yet there was also something vaguely collegiate about an apparent 'appreciation' of trad. Before 'ACKER' was studded on the backs of proletariat leather jackets where 'ELVIS' once was, it was mostly the property of undergraduates flirting with bohemia before becoming teachers.

At student union dances, they'd show off how grown-up they were by donning boaters or top hats, and a variety of hacked-about formal gear, drinking heavily of cider and launching into vigorous steps that blended a kind of skip-jiving with the Charleston in a curious galumphing motion to 'When The Saints Go Marching In', 'Down By The Riverside', 'Swanee River' or, for gawd's sake, 'Bobby Shaftoe', arranged for the plinking and puffing of a trad band like The Pagan Jazzmen in Newcastle – in which an Eric Burdon slid trombone – or Ed O'Donnell's New Orleans Jazzmen, pride of Leeds, whose maiden bash at Halifax's Plebians Jazz Club was bruited by student enthusiasts parading the streets in sandwich boards. The same equation as that linking Elvis Presley with Vince Eager existed between British and North American trad dads: you'd never beat the Yanks, but you could have fun and even make a little money displaying your inferiority complex.

Thus, after an enforced absence of two years' National Service in the navy, trumpeter John Keen was astonished in 1957 to find that the Cheltenham trad-jazz scene had exploded: 'You could go and hear it every night of the week. Rock-and-roll and rhythm-and-blues weren't considered important at all, and the only guitar group that anyone had heard of were The Shadows, who were really a show band with their funny walks and gimmicks.'[4]

Home-reared trad performers tussled for work within easy reach in village institutes, pub function rooms, dance halls, sports pavilions and whenever the Alstone Baths was boarded over for such a purpose. In the town centre, the places to see and be seen were the Black Tulip, the Rotunda, St Luke's Hall, pubs such as the Star, the Cat And Fiddle, the Gladstone Arms and the Eight Bells and coffee bars like the Tiffin, Bar-B-Q, Waikiki, the Patio Snack Bar, El Flamenco – which were sometimes booking trad bands as a change from the jukebox.[5]

Yet, while trad was in the ascendant, many skifflers who were contemplating whether or not to donate their Lonnie Donegan 78s to jumble sales backslid gradually, via wary amplification, to rock 'n' roll – 'a more commercial form of skiffle', shrugged the authors of 1960's unconsciously humorous *A Guide To Popular Music*[6] – and an increasingly more American UK Top 20. Nevertheless, rejecting the hit-parade detritus that people knew and wanted to dance to, certain music lovers were to begin polarising their tastes in black Americana rather than pursue Woody Guthrie, Cisco Houston and other white folk singers who had impressed leading skifflers like Donegan, Dickie Bishop and Wally Whyton.

A case study of such a consumer might be Surbiton schoolboy Chris Dreja, who 'taught myself boogie-woogie piano on the family upright, but I bought an acoustic guitar for five shillings [25p/40c] from a local pawn shop. The strings were about an inch [2.5cm] off the fretboard, but it gave me incredible strength and steadiness in my left hand. My best friend, Tony "Top" Topham's Dad had all these great import blues records – Blind Lemon Jefferson, Robert Johnson... They kept me awake for days on end, just thinking about them – and I went ballistic when I heard the electric sounds of Jimmy Reed.'

As rabid a devotee of the acoustic blues ingredient in skiffle's melting pot was Brian Jones – for whom the stuff mutated too into a craving, almost a religion. He was to be especially taken with the grippingly personal styles of rural bluesmen like Snooks Eaglin, Champion Jack Dupree,[7] Robert Johnson and the equally inventive Lightning Hopkins as well as Huddie 'Leadbelly' Leadbetter and one-man-band Jesse Fuller; the latter both absorbed a boundless repertoire embracing not only blues – Leadbelly's 'devil's ditties' – but also country square dance and children's play rhymes.

Like Chris Dreja, Brian had also taught himself to play acoustic six-string, but he'd also developed the beginnings of a naive personal style on alto saxophone based on his knowledge of the clarinet, also in the woodwind family.

Even with GCE O-levels looming, Brian was 'sitting in' non-committally with parochial outfits who were semi-professional at best with too few bookings to stay the chill of workaday reality. How did you get up to the next level, living so far away from London – then as now the epicentre of the British music industry – and outside the geographical limit of the pool where the kingdom's four major record labels were prepared to fish for talent? The mountains had to come to Mohammed, and back-of-beyond entertainers in Cheltenham who didn't head east had to be content with weekend evenings where, through latticed windows dim with grime, they'd be perceived setting up puny amplifiers to power never-never electric guitars and voices yet to spit out the plum.

'It would seem to have the characteristics of a temporary craze,' sniffed *A Guide To Popular Music* of rock 'n' roll, 'rather than the more lasting folk element of skiffle.'[6] Always, it was never too late to give up 'music' – if that's what you called it – and concentrate on exams or try for a raise and even promotion, instead of just waiting for Friday to roll around, but who wanted to keep his nose clean and slip into a 'cushy' position and henceforth into dull and respectable old age when there remained even the possibility of a more glamorous alternative, no matter how remote?

Brian Jones didn't. Bitten by the skiffle bug, he'd formed a combo so short-lived that it never made a public appearance. Nevertheless, he held sway over it as Lonnie Donegan did over the entire movement. While Lonnie was its wellspring, it was possible to perceive vaguely regional hues of skiffle, largely through folk traditions leaving their mark. In the West, acts such as Ray Bush And His Avon Cities Skiffle and Salisbury's Satellites betrayed ancestry in morris dance sides via their employment of squeeze-boxes.

Like punk after it, any provincial oik who'd mastered basic techniques could have a crack at skiffle – and the more ingenuous the sound, the better. Percussion and chords slashed on an acoustic guitar were at the core of its contagious backbeat, and no one had howled with derision at a washboard tapped with thimbles, broomstick bass, dustbin-lid cymbals, biscuit-tin snare drum and further vehicles of musical effect fashioned from household implements.

Such displays had been generally for the benefit of performers rather than onlookers, but the proprietor of the Odeon, Cheltenham's principal cinema, interspersed movies like *Tarzan And The Lost Safari*, *Idle On Parade* and the latest Norman Wisdom with occasional in-person performances by amateurs, including groups fronted by youths enjoying fleeting moments of make-believing they were Lonnie or Elvis.

By late 1959, however, Donegan appeared to be on the wane, if still capable of pulling unexpected commercial strokes, and Presley was square-bashing as a drafted US soldier in Germany. More to the point, Cheltenham's first homogenous rock 'n' roll ensembles were barring themselves from dances at the staider youth clubs as well as the stuffy dinner-and-dances upon which they might have depended for virtually all paid work had they traded in 'decent' music.

This was in the heartland of a prudish Britain that had hounded babysnatching Jerry Lee Lewis from its shores in 1958, and was to oblige Billy Fury to moderate his Presley-esque gyrations. Moreover, Gloucester city burghers had barred an Evesham ensemble, The Sapphires, from ever defiling its Guildhall again because lead vocalist Rodney Dawes' trousers were deemed 'crude' round the thighs and crotch.

Cheltenham's boss groups were The Talismen – winners, years later, of a readers' popularity poll in *Midland Beat*, in case you're wondering where you'd heard of them – and the older Ramrods, a quintet whose standardised name might have caused confusion had they advanced beyond parochial engagements.[8] In a monochrome publicity photograph taken in St Mary's churchyard, The Ramrods differentiated between the instrumentalists – the usual two guitarists, bass player and drummer – and Philip Crowther, a four-eyed singer, distinguished by a light-coloured jacket in contrast to the others' darker ones, though all sported black bowties against white shirts.

As it was with, say, Dave Dee and The Bostons in Salisbury, Pete Mystery And His Strangers in Andover and another Sapphires in

Dartmouth – who wore their town's coat of arms on their uniform blazers – The Ramrods were to Cheltenham what Cliff Richard and The Shadows were to television. Yet, though Phil Crowther might have proved a passable Cliff, the rest desired to sound less like The Shadows than Duane Eddy, New York-born pioneer of the 'twangy guitar' approach, who boomed his instrumentals solely on his echo-chambered guitar's lower strings. 'Rebel Rouser', 1958's 'Ramrod' and further of Eddy and his backing Rebels' many hits also showcased a saxophone melody in counterpoint.

There came, therefore, overtures from The Ramrods for Brian Jones to join them, and two equally plausible but opposing accounts of his involvement. According to Pat Andrews, he attended a mere couple of rehearsals, but Barry Miles, entertainments secretary at the art college, maintained that 'the local band I always hired for our dances, was The Ramrods – which had Brian Jones on saxophone'.[9]

Bespectacled, taper-thin and of bohemian persuasion, Barry – who encouraged people to address him by his surname – disliked Brian intensely, partly because Jones was something of a sexual braggart to the extent of being regarded by some as a total fantasist. With the oral contraceptive Conovid – 'the pill' – not yet in UK chemists' stockrooms, premarital congress was as big a step to take before the Sixties started Swinging as it would be when AIDS and like ailments put on the brake as the millennium loomed. Condoms – 'rubber johnnies' – still burst, and 'pulling out' was even less of a guarantee that you wouldn't have to either 'do the decent thing', procure a backstreet abortionist or leave the girl and your conscience in the lurch.

To sceptical cronies, a changing-room lothario at Cheltenham Grammar would brag, therefore, of carnal capers that everybody imagined were tall tales. He might have got to 'third base' after a lot of effort, but only a 'cheap' girl didn't 'save herself' for her future husband.

However, in an era when boys were spotty and girls untouchable, there was not exactly evidence, but reluctant educated guesses, that Brian Jones, a most heterosexual young man, was actually getting away with more romantic conquests than most – which may have led green-eyed monsters to whisper to his detractors. It helped that he looked a bit like Adam Faith, the latest pretender to Cliff Richard's crown, with his firm jawline, gaunt Viking cheekbones and brushed-forward greaseless haircut.

Faith's seven-year chart run had left the starting line with two Number ones, followed by a Number Two with 1960's 'Someone Else's Baby'. He was to ascend to such national celebrity that a 1961 edition of *Hancock's Half Hour* would have the late comedian grousing, 'There's Adam Faith earning ten times as much as the Prime Minister. Is that right? Mind you, I suppose it depends on whether you like Adam Faith or what your politics are.'[10]

As 'Terry Denver', Adam had first flickered from the Ravenswood television set, strumming guitar with The Worried Men on BBC's *Six-Five Special*, a series that just about passed muster with Lewis and Louise because producer Jack Good's old-maidish superiors had obliged him to balance the pop with string quartets, features on sports and purposeful hobbies, and such upstanding interlocutors as former boxing champion Freddie Mills. This brief also allowed trad jazz and, less frequently, ethnic blues by visiting black North Americans such as Big Bill Broonzy, whose vocal lines were fired by the impetus of a then-novel 12-string guitar. *Teleclub*, too, was 'a magazine programme for the under twenty-ones', containing as it did 'acts by young professional entertainers, sport, interest, a personal problem, and your turn'[11] with music directed by the avuncular Steve Race. When Independent Television (ITV) began in 1956, the inclusion of Humphrey Lyttelton's Jazz Band on *Round About Ten*, shortly before the *Epilogue*, was as racy as it got.

Needless to say, Brian was to become an avid watcher, whenever he could, of those few TV broadcasts containing what could be described as pop. The BBC Light Programme was also directed principally at the old and square – though *Saturday Club*, a two-hour pop show, was on the horizon; Cy Grant's calypsos enlivened Cliff Michelmore's topical *Tonight* and on *Radio Rhythm Club* 'there'd be one "folk song" per programme,' remembered Lonnie Donegan. 'Sometimes it was a blues.' Sometimes, too, it was sung with a resident vocalist's plummy gentility when surfacing on *Services Calling*, an Entertainments National Service Association (ENSA) series, in which such a version of 'Down The Road

Apiece' – owing as much to C&W as blues in the 1941 hit arrangement by Ray McKinley – was introduced by interlocutor Sally Douglas as a 'good old good one'..

Brian may have been told by someone at school or else tuned into it by accident, but it became his habit to fall out of bed at five on selected mornings to catch a half-hour blues show on the American Forces Network. Through the static, too, came the British Forces Network (BFN), whose opening transmission from Hamburg in 1946 had coincided with the inauguration of the Light Programme. Ploughing a light entertainment furrow, too, BFN staff included such future denizens of BBC Broadcasting House as Cliff Michelmore, Brian Matthew – host of *Saturday Club* – and Alexis Korner, later cited as 'the father of British blues', who moonlighted as presenter with Nordwestdeutsche Rundfunk – closed down in 1955 – and was recalled by Michelmore for his expeditions 'in search of jazz along the Reeperbahn'.[12]

A red-light district since the days of three-mast clippers, Hamburg's Reeperbahn bore as much relation to the most eye-stretching of Cheltenham's GI recreations as dairy butter does to low-fat margarine. Illicit sex seemed to be in its infancy amongst the civilian population, too. Nevertheless, Brian Jones was well on the way to completing his first sexual pilgrimage by the time his O-level results – he'd passed all nine of them – fluttered onto the Hatherley Road doormat. Through some undignified gropings, he'd ascertained that even a church youth club's most arch proto-feminist – the sort that looked as if she couldn't wait for a chess tournament, followed by a natter about the transmutation of souls – might be screaming for sex as much as any pimpled bloke.

Every effort by his parents to nip in the bud anything untoward in Brian was in vain. Already, it had been necessary to distance him from Barbara – with whom Louise found a perverse pleasure in gossiping about her son's real and imagined transgressions.

You only had to look at him to tell what he was like. Take when he started growing his hair Adam Faith length – maybe a centimetre or two (inch or so) beyond the short-back-and-sides limit that marked sobriety and masculinity. His father added this to a list of complaints about what he perceived as the school's lax discipline – that, as Brian grew more burly, he was less able to enforce himself – during too-frequent and fraught discussions with a heavily patient Dr Bell.

An especially distressing failure to live up to Lewis's expectations was Brian's now open rejection of dictates about what was and wasn't 'good' music. It made no difference that fledglings from the upper classes were ardent jazz fans – as instanced by the Queen's cousin, the Hon Gerald Lascelles, who edited a book on the subject and the 21-year-old Earl of Wharncliffe, who'd joined the Musicians' Union in 1956 in order to drum with a Sheffield jazz band.

At best, a passion for any type of pop music would bring puffy smiles to the lips of the most open-minded do-gooders in cardigans who presided over botany, charity work, the Great Outdoors and further hearty pastimes intended to distract young minds from what Robert Baden-Powell described in *Scouting For Boys* as 'the secret vice of beastliness'. [13] When not inside St Mary's youth club for ping pong and 'Brains Trusts' on current affairs, you could be out brass rubbing or booting a muddy piece of leather about.

Despite himself, Brian was sound enough at sport, particularly badminton and cricket – both far less dangerous than football – a drag of a game, especially at school when winter twilight descended, and lights were switched on in the classrooms. He was also a strong swimmer, spending most of his week's suspension for the prefect insurrection at the Alstone Baths that, as well as aquatic pursuits, was an avenue for precipitating an onset of 'beastliness' through observing the semi-naked female form.

The rising sap of puberty had led him to dwell, too, on fast flashes of knicker when, at parties, teenage dances and like forums, girls jived round their handbags with ruby-red lips, tight sweaters, wide belts and ponytails, making believe that they were as elfin as Audrey Hepburn in *Roman Holiday* (which reached Cheltenham a full year after its London premiere).

The immediate subtext of Brian's yet unspoken fancy, that he'd like to make his way in the world as a musician, was that it might procure him readier access to more than a fumble at a bra strap than most of the other fellows who'd paid half a crown (12^1/2p/20c) to mooch about with an inbuilt sense of defeat in the gloom beyond the burning footlights.

It might have been a shadowy link to higher cultural expression to some, but the strongest motive for even the most ill-favoured youth, let alone one as handsome as Brian Jones, was licence to make eye contact with gawking 'birds' ringing the stage front, ogling with unmaidenly eagerness the enigma of untouchable boys next door. A tryst during an intermission could be sealed with a grin, a flood of libido and an, 'All right, then. I'll see you later.' If his parents were out for the evening or, better still, gone for the weekend, Brian could bring a girl back for 'coffee' afterwards. She could drink it in his bedroom – or in his bed if she liked.

The atmosphere at home had intensified. There was nothing as yet to indicate possibilities other than in secure but dead-end jobs with a gold watch on retirement to tick away the seconds before you went underground. Attempts by Brian to discuss a different future with Lewis would prove pointless. Variations on the same theme of prevarication would just come up over and over again, and end, as likely as not, with a blazing row. Trying to elicit his mother's sympathy only brought to the fore how little she ever considered not only what his ambitions might be, but whether he even had any. Eventually, hardly a word would pass between parents and child that wasn't a domestic imperative, and by the time Brian reached the Upper Sixth he was almost permanently out of the house.

To his parents' mingled delight and exasperation, he was to gain GCE A-levels in Chemistry and Physics. This was an excellent result, all things considered – for Brian's heart had been heavy with fear and guilt in the weeks leading up to those days of days.

The trouble – the biggest he had ever been in – started at a party held one Friday night in 1958, when the host's parents were away overnight. The living room had been transformed into a den of iniquity by dimming table lamps with headscarves and pushing back armchairs as a prelude to snogging and attacks of 'desert sickness'.[14] The soundtrack to this effused from the Dansette record player in the corner, surrounded by a scattering of brittle 78s and the plastic 45rpm discs that were superseding them.

It was in this exotic scenario that Brian, pushy and confident with Devon cider, first noticed the coltish charms of a softly spoken schoolgirl three years his junior, sitting amongst a prattle of her friends. By circuitous and nonchalant inquiry, he learned from the other fellows that her name was Valerie, but no one knew if she went all the way or was hanging onto her virginity. Conversely, Valerie, if feigning indifference, seemed to be weighing up Brian out of the corner of her eye.

Contact was established before the evening was out, and conversation over the din of the Dansette emboldened Brian to plant an exploratory kiss on Valerie's lips. Then, to use a tabloid expression, further intimacy took place. Yet, as he recounted to the lads later, she wasn't exactly 'a hole in one'. Nevertheless, during subsequent frolics over the next few weeks, matters took a serious and abandoned turn and, if Brian had come prepared, caution was outweighed by the thrilling few seconds of extra-sensitive and exquisite orgasm a torn condom afforded him.

Pregnancy wasn't what happened to girls like Valerie, or boys from the same social class like Brian. Such carelessness was the way of 'common' youths, who were then obliged to go through with a wedding ceremony portrayed falsely by the baby's grandparents as the outcome of a sudden love match between their daughter and the dashing young plumber's mate.

It was the most ruinous of all British social disgraces, a stain that was as indelible as Lady Macbeth's damned spot. As late as 1969, Anne Allen, a *Sunday Mirror* columnist assured readers that, 'It is rotten to be born illegitimate. Statistics clearly show that illegitimate babies are more likely to be born dead than other babies or destined for a very short life.'

Headlined 'STIGMA THAT LASTS A LIFETIME', it supplied further erroneous details: 'They are more often ill and they have more accidents. They live in worse conditions than most of us. They are often poorer than everyone else around them, and this can occasionally be because the local Ministry of Social Security gives them a little less than it has the power to do – almost as though it was punishing mother and child.'[15]

In Ireland, 'fallen women' and girls who had 'asked' to be raped or merely looked as if they might give in to nature's baser urges could, with the full approval of parents and Church, be incarcerated and forced into what amounted to near enough slave labour in Magdalen Asylums, a network of vast laundries run by the so-called Sisters of Mercy, an order of nuns. The last one closed in 1996.[16]

For young unmarried fathers, no matter how high the percentage of fault, the repercussions were less onerous – sometimes no more than admonitions along the lines of 'You've had your fun and now you must pay for it' – and that wasn't necessarily the case if the brat was adopted. Nevertheless, as far as the Jones family's parish circle of bring-and-buy sales, nativity plays and tombolas was concerned, Brian could blow Weber's *Clarinet Concerto* and pass A-levels for the next hundred years and yet never wipe out the memory of Valerie and the baby.

On receiving the news that her period was a month overdue, Brian had groped for reasons why the truth need not inflict itself upon him. As he and Valerie didn't even like each other much anyway, he tried to avoid the issue by avoiding her, especially after she'd told him she'd been sick that morning. He promised her that that was probably because of extreme anxiety. That her waist was a few centimetres bigger might be nothing either, although she said her wrists, armpits and ankles felt a bit peculiar.

With the same questions surfacing over and over again, he'd build up a damning case against himself before concluding that he was panicking unduly. However, as the days crawled by, there came no 'splashdown', and he was seeing prams and big-bellied women everywhere, in the streets and in public parks, and even hearing them on the radio. In a repeat, on the BBC Home Service, of Dylan Thomas's *Under Milk Wood: A Play For Voices* – to which his parents listened with observed reverence – there was an unmarried mother named Polly Garter. She spoke a bit like Valerie.

Brian could no longer not believe it. There was an urban myth that some struck-off quack in Bristol performed abortions for sixty quid ($100) – which might be negotiable. Then again Valerie could talc her face ghostly white and make her eyes enormous so she'd look sick enough for the local doctor or his second opinion to prescribe getting rid of it legally. Were they allowed to do that nowadays?

Such speculation was academic, because Valerie would not hear of an abortion or pay heed to perilous advice about making yourself miscarry with gin and a hot bath. No, she intended to tell her parents. Brian, therefore, could not postpone breaking the news to his.

It was the first of many Worst Moments of his life. He'd pondered doing it somewhere crowded like the market, where his mother couldn't pretend to have hysterics. People would stare – and that would never do. She suspected already that something was up, and was no longer mistaking his frequent brown studies for adolescent sullenness.

A mist of resigned despair shrouded Ravenswood. Lewis and Louise had been too appalled to erupt with anger. Moreover, having come out with it at last, Brian became like a detached spectator with no interest or stake in the situation. His and Valerie's parents could sort it out between them, while the riptide of the drama washed over him. Besides, he had to revise for A-levels.

With no crucial exams pending, Valerie was packed off to a faraway aunt's and then to a 'home' where the baby – a boy – was taken away from her as soon as he was born, and delivered as arranged to an infertile couple. A legitimate and all-embracing colour had been given to her non-attendance at school for the best part of two terms. She was, insisted her parents, recovering from 'a nervous breakdown'.[17]

As for Brian, he'd been sent to obliging acquaintances of his parents in Germany for a chaperoned six weeks. What a holiday that must have been, but it was deemed necessary after the vapourings of the town's scandalmongers – via the *Gloucestershire Echo* – reached the ears of the muck-raking *News Of The World*, who commissioned a nicotine-fingered doorstepper to investigate this rare instance of moral indiscretion that lurked in refined Cheltenham. He was stonewalled by Mr and Mrs Jones, who'd put it about that Brian's summer sojourn in the Fatherland was his reward for getting high grades in the jolly old A-levels.

3 Beatnik Fly

'He was a reformed traddie, and, although he despised them, he was really one of them.'

– Mick Jagger [1]

When it became clear that it was all over bar the shouting, Brian didn't find the furore entirely unpleasant. There was, he discovered, a certain cachet in being as illustrious for his sexual athletics as his prowess as a musician – so much so that, later, he was to acquire a myth-gilding mascot in a small stuffed goat.

He was, therefore, vaguely disappointed that his return from exile in early autumn aroused little inquisitiveness. No one asked disagreeable questions, and, though the escapade would be brought up now and then by peevish and prying parents in the comfort of their own home, adult neighbours and St Mary's parishioners pretended at least that they accepted the party line about a holiday treat.

To Lewis and Louise, the reproaches and comparisons to children who were a credit to their families seemed to be having the desired effect. Brian seemed contrite, slightly traumatised and disconcertingly keen to make amends by going to the barber's, even attending church without fuss, dressing with baggy reticence and conducting himself generally as a model (if rather reserved) son.

In town-centre coffee bars and student pubs, however, he was more of an unknown quantity, now that he was no longer a uniformed sixth-former. Precise fact had dissipated to a generalised suspicion that that blond bloke had some kind of skeleton in the cupboard. He was quite willing to talk about it in detail if asked, although he turned the visit to

Germany into a freewheeling trek around Scandinavia with his guitar on his back, a vagabond troubadour playin' the simple, unaffected kinda music folk like a-tappin' their boot leather to.

As well as the rural blues end of skiffle, this included, he told them, the canons of black performers who'd migrated from the cotton-picking Deep South to southside Chicago. He dropped names like Howlin' Wolf, Muddy Waters, Brownie McGhee and others from the pages that nobody else read in *Melody Maker*. No one listening was sure whether to challenge Brian either when he said that, if requested, he was also capable of the unpolished Dust Bowl ramblings of Woody Guthrie – and ditties from the Appalachian highlands, where, he elucidated, early British settlers had stabilised a conservative repertoire that, with minimum melodic variations – the formal opposite of jazz – had persisted for centuries. Perhaps the best-known item from this source was 'Go And Tell Aunt Nancy', which cropped up in the boundless repertoire of walking archive Leadbelly.

Leading as eventful a life as Leadbelly was Johnny Cash, a country and western (C&W) singer whose music, with its plain riffs and clockwork rhythms, Brian had come to like too. After all, in its blending of cowboy pessimism and Victorian broadness of gesture, what else is C&W if not white-trash blues? What else would Johnny be but a blurred role model of a kind for Brian in a then-unimagined future?

Arkansas-born Cash was the principal country specialist on Sun, the record label founded in Memphis, Tennessee 'the home of the blues', which had hit the jackpot when Elvis Presley came by in 1954. With his low-down bass growl and facial scar, Johnny was too butch to be one more Elvis but, after his first crop of Sun hits, he began a strenuous round of engagements in the Deep South stretching over a year ahead. After the initial leg of poorly paid bookings – some hundreds of kilometres apart – it dawned on Cash what a joyless grind now blighted his life. This irreversible imposition caused the itinerary to degenerate into a subsidised booze-up laced with amphetamines. Giggling drunk or on another planet, introspective Johnny became an erratic performer, walking a line between rubbish and dazed inspiration.

Advisedly, you'd find no mention of this in Cash press releases, but Brian's essentially scholarly nature dictated delving as far as he was able beneath the show-business veneer of the musicians he admired. Almost as if he was embroiled in formal research, he voyaged evening after evening into the small hours, cataloguing and gloating over his growing collection of vinyl treasures, finding much to notice, study and compare in sleeve notes, composer credits and so on. Hardly any piece of information was too insignificant to be less than totally absorbing in the weekly music press, too, especially *Melody Maker*, which covered jazz and blues as well as mainstream pop.

He wasn't that far removed from an obsessed supporter of a football team. He had taken his blues fixation in particular so far that he cared no more about how others might have mocked it than a chimp in the zoo does about what the public looking through the bars thinks about its antics. Brian bought Paul Oliver's *Blues Fell This Morning*, then a standard work,[2] as soon as it was published in 1960, turning to it as a monk to the Bible, working his way through as much of its bibliography that could be ordered from the library, and fanning out to erudite tomes concerning, say, plantation field hollers and the African roots of blues.

He could dwell very eloquently and with great authority on this and lesser interests when, for the price of a transparent cup of frothy coffee, he sat for hours on end, chatting with other teenagers in the Aztec café, above a high street shop. This rendezvous modelled itself on the Gyre and Gimble, the 2I's, the Safari and like venues over the edge of the world in central London, where the likes of Harry Webb, Brian Rankin and Reg Smith used to entertain before changing their respective names to Cliff Richard, Hank Marvin and Marty Wilde.

Thus the Aztec had been transformed with newly painted walls, bench seats, kidney-shaped tables, wine-bottle candle-holders, dangling fishing nets, a jukebox and an espresso machine.

Fifteen-year-old Patricia Andrews worked behind the counter three or four evenings a week after days in class at Christchurch School for Girls. With deceptive casualness, she entered the life of Brian Jones, after a mutual acquaintance arranged a blind date at the Aztec. Her first impression of him was offputting, as he was wearing a brown herringbone tweed double-breasted suit, all elephant folds in the trousers – possibly one of his father's castoffs. Worse, Pat had been warned that he was shy and quietly spoken – which was at odds with his fading notoriety over the Valerie business. He was certainly extremely polite, standing up to greet her with outstretched hand and deferential smile. The only trick he missed was clicking his heels and bowing like a Prussian hussar.

His recent experience abroad was common ground, as Pat was still in touch with a German boyfriend who'd been working in Cheltenham until a family bereavement had brought him home. The rest of the evening was plain sailing, as Brian was not coy after all 'but all in all, a nice, gentle sort of person'. Beamed Pat, 'He was capable of discussing all different subjects without seeming to be a know-all.'

Brian in turn was bewitched by Pat's svelte profile, avalanche of wavy brown hair and the deceptive command in a timorously pretty face. He invited her to the cinema the following Saturday to see X-certificate *Never Take Sweets From A Stranger*. The next day, Brian ate Sunday lunch with the Andrews family – with whom he was a palpable hit.

'He impressed my two elder brothers with his knowledge of modern jazz,' remembered Pat, 'my sister because she said he was such a perfect gentleman and my parents with his praise for my mother's cooking and his willingness to wash the dishes – because all the men in our house had been brought up not to do domestic chores like that.'

A rumbustious and enormous Sunday meal with starters, roast meat and pudding was unknown at Ravenswood – 'something to do with not toiling (which included cooking) on the Sabbath,' said Pat – where the only safe noises were the unavoidable clatterings of cutlery on plate. Brian also savoured affection rather than antagonism in the affable home of a sweetheart whom his own parents would judge to be no better than she ought to be.

Pat, see, was 'working class', a new arrival whose forebears had appeared in census rolls in London's East End since dray horses had dragged cargos onto merchants vessels poised to catch the Thames tide. She was the only member of her family who hadn't been born a Cockney. Into the bargain, Patricia Andrews was a 'shop girl', shortly to move from the Aztec to full-time counter assistant at Boots the Chemists. As a similar position in Curry's record shop was among his various and fleeting jobs after leaving school – and, soon afterwards, after leaving home, too – Brian might have argued that he was a 'shop boy', but he had long become used to keeping his opinions to himself at Ravenswood. Otherwise, it only caused trouble.

Serving customers at Curry's was more socially acceptable to Louise and Lewis than some of the more distressing occupations for which Brian was overqualified – as a coalman, on the night shift in an ice-cream factory – and, for goodness sake, for all the world to see in the uniform of a bus conductor after he'd been found wanting as an office junior in the architectural department of Cheltenham District Council.

However much his mother wrung her hands – 'You have broken mine and your father's hearts' was a recurring sentence – and Lewis prevailed upon him to see sense, Pat understood that humdrum day jobs were incidental to Brian's principal vocational purpose. He was worthy of pride rather than chastisement and criticism – because, glowed Pat, 'at that age, to be able to say to your friends, "Guess what my boyfriend does? He's a really talented musician," was really nice.'

The romance ran smoothly at first, even after he filched small change from Pat's handbag to buy cigarettes; ripped up an airmail letter containing photos from her German admirer ('That was the first time I saw Brian lose his temper') and blew a month's wages on a down payment for an electric guitar.

Brian's lackadaisical attitude towards the accumulation of debt had been exacerbated by his parents' unwillingness to act as guarantors for hire-purchase instalments for what they considered to be wanton caprices. This would, they felt, imply approval of his increasing divergence from the straight-and-narrow. Perhaps a hand-to-mouth existence for a while would drive a discomfited Brian back to the fold via application form or supplicatory telephone call. While he was in the mood, he might also get rid of those corrupting records and let the HP firm repossess the electrical junk that was at the root of his continued stupidity.

Therefore, waiting, like Mr Micawber, for something to turn up, Brian was forever devising means of scrounging the wherewithal to keep body and soul together. He would fiddle petty cash from the Curry's till; strike up shallow acquaintance with any mug with a pocketful of money in hopes of a loan or a free meal and organise 'rent parties', charging admission and collecting the money back on empty bottles.

Whilst still owing rent in previous flats and lodgings, he was now living on the first floor of 73 Prestbury Road, five minutes' dawdle from the High Street. He shared a double bedroom with Richard Hattrell, a young man five years his senior. Richard's immediate family were from the legal and military professions. His had been a privileged upbringing, albeit one that had been as bleak after its fashion as Brian's. Enduring the rigours of expensive boarding schools before finishing his education at Tewkesbury Secondary Modern, he was also saddled with an overbearing army colonel of a father who, sighed Richard 'went berserk when he found out I was a jazz fan'.

Indeed, Richard had noticed Brian Jones one Thursday during a show starring Kenny Ball's Jazzmen at the Rotunda, a venue along the Promenade. However, the two first spoke at length at Club 66, a suburban jazz stronghold. Brian had been going there since 1958 and, as its appointed secretary, endorsed Richard's membership card, signing it 'LB Jones'.

That night, the bill was top-heavy with trad. Tony Mann's modern ensemble opened proceedings for Bill Nile's Delta Jazz Band, The Chelt Valley Stompers and an outfit led by trumpeter John Keen, who deviated from ordained Dixieland precedent by including saxophonists and committing the more cardinal sin of amplification, to the disgruntlement of watching devotees likely to know more about the music's history than the musicians – so much so that the 'jazz' content in numbers by certain local bands was frequently negligible because, if some black dotard from New Orleans had recorded a particularly definitive solo, it was often thought prudent to learn it note for note for regurgitation at every public performance.

The more incensed purists might boo, but John Keen not sticking to the rules was a point in his favour to Brian Jones – who said as much when introduced to Keen at 38 Priory Street, the family home of Jane Philby, who, with a team of helpers, had spent most of the summer of 1958 converting the basement into a café-cum-party-venue for local musicians and their retinues. 'Then a stage was set up,' recalled John

Keen, 'and the place flourished. It was a gathering of like-minded people in their late teens and early twenties.'[3]

Before this development, entertainment had effused from Jane's record player. Pretending to be 'sent' by Lewis, Meade Lux rather than Lewis, Jerry Lee, the eyes of cross-legged patrons closed in ecstasy at the sheer joy of being anarchistic, free-loving and pacifist – or at least being seen to sound and look as if they were. There were places like it in nearly every town in the country. Amused by the memory, Reading's Mike Cooper reconjured how Marianne Faithfull, then attending a local Convent school, 'used to come to the house we had in Silver Street for guitar lessons. She was hanging out in the local coffee bars in her yellow-and-brown school uniform.

'We actually got raided by the drug squad. I was in the kitchen shaving, and suddenly these policemen appeared in the back garden, and someone was knocking on the back-door at the same time. They completely ransacked the place, and took away my hay-fever tablets. They didn't find anything else because none of use even smoked dope in those days. I think, however, that they were a bit shocked at the postmodern squalor we lived in. We were beatniks, man!'

Jane Philby would not have her parents offended by any condemnation of 38 Priory Road as a house of ill-repute, but, while it did not attract unwelcome attention from the Gloucestershire constabulary, inadequate soundproofing meant that the high Cs from John Keen's horn would stab the night air in surrounding streets at a time before phrases like 'noise pollution' and 'environmental health' had been coined.

More insidious was the sound of Brian Jones's guitar fed through an amplifier purchased for his use by John Keen, 'a Vox AC15 for thirty pounds [$50] from Ray Electrical in the Lower High Street. Brian put his acoustic guitar fitted with a pick-up through it. He never paid me back, by the way. He was very keen on the way Freddie Green, the guitarist with Count Basie, played. Very tasteful. Brian was a good jazz rhythm guitarist, and used to sit in with us, Bill Nile and visitors from London such as The Alex Welsh Band.'[3]

Welsh and his boys were respected rather than popular, partly because they disregarded the matching Donegal tweeds, Confederate army uniforms, Roman togas, barrister wigs and similarly ridiculous variations on the striped waistcoats and bowlers worn by Acker Bilk And His Paramount Jazz Band, forever on *Trad Tavern*, a series occupying the air-time once filled by *Six-Five Special* and its less pious ITV successor, *Oh Boy!*. Musically, too, every other trad band on the show was different, every one was the same: banjos, a confusion of horns and 'dads' who imagined that a hoarse monotone was all you needed to sing like Louis Armstrong.

It was beneath Brian Jones to dress up in some silly costume to play trad. Neither had he any qualms about walking off if the band launched into 'Down By The Riverside', 'Bobby Shaftoe' or any instance of leather-elbowed, clipped-bearded and insufferably square 'teacher music'. While he half-enjoyed the soft fret-board swing of Wes Montgomery, Brian, like Freddie Green, took solos rarely. Yet he was solidly at the music's heart, ministering to the overall effect – which would have been weaker without him.

For this reason, there were incidents reported of other players uniting in roundabout persuasion and then naked pleas for Brian to return to the stage after a beer break, no matter how petulantly he behaved up there. Defiance, hesitation and final agreement might have chased across his face, but if he got as far as the wings there was no assurance that he wouldn't bolt at the last second. Conversely, he often had every intention of acquiescing, but, effervescent with malicious glee, enjoyed being the centre of offstage attention as opposed to skulking beyond the main spotlight on the boards.

'Brian despised certain aspects of the jazz scene,' confirmed John Keen. 'On a personal level, he could certainly charm people, but he was a jazz snob in some ways, and could be uncooperative. When we were onstage, he just wouldn't play some numbers if he thought they were old hat. He was also unreliable and just didn't turn up for gigs if he couldn't be bothered.'[3]

When circumstances were favourable, Jones's chord-strumming and *obbligatos* were controlled but lively, and his relocation via Freddie Green of eight-to-the-bar banjo to electric rhythm guitar in the Cheltenham trad days was to be lasting and beneficial, leaving its mark on, for example,

'It's All Over Now', 'You Can't Catch Me' and '19th Nervous Breakdown' by The Rolling Stones.

Yet, while playing parochial trad now could fill every evening of the week, Brian was fundamentally of Tony Mann's 'modern' persuasion – which, in his terms, embraced the mainstream orchestral euphoria of Basie and Ellington; the white swing of Woody Herman and Benny Goodman and the blaring bebop of Charlie Mingus, the harder Jazz Messengers and Charlie 'Yardbird' Parker. Strewn about the Prestbury Road flat, too, were LPs recorded under Parker's spell by Ornette Coleman, Roland Kirk and, especially, alto and soprano saxophonist Julian Edwin 'Cannonball' Adderley.

On instant replay for weeks at a time was Brian's dog-eared 1958 album *Somethin' Else* by Adderley, and assembled hard boppers including Miles Davis and drummer Art Blakey. At its worst, some of the textural complexities of *Somethin' Else* and later Adderley LPs either reminded you of that 'party sequence' music that dates 'modern times' continental movies made over and over again since the late 1950s – or sounded very Light Programme, as exemplified on the 1963 single, 'The Sidewalks Of New York', which was dominated by the too-pure tone of a vibraphone.

Yet elsewhere, it bordered on that jazzy pop that was acceptable to hip circles in Cheltenham, Reading and other points en route to London, notably through Adderley's mingling of state-of-the-art jazz with elements of Louis Jordan, Cab Calloway and other pre-Presley executants of a jovial and danceable hybrid of trad and jump-blues.

Adderley's composition 'Sack O' Woe' was to surface as a British R&B 'standard', being recorded by Manfred Mann, The Rats[4] and Van Morrison – and, as late as 2001, electric organist Brian Auger, a sort of godfather of acid jazz, was inspired to write a track for a new album '[when] I woke up one morning with this little theme running through my head. What the hell was it? I thought, "I know this, but I don't." After racking my brain all day, I realized that it was the reverse of "Azule Serape", which is on a Cannonball Adderley album – a number featuring Victor Feldman, his pianist.'

Far from the wheezy Magnificats in St Mary's as Adderley, too, was the fluid organ beneath the hands of 'Brother' Jack McDuff and, later,

Jimmy Smith, Richard 'Groove' Holmes and Booker T. Ray Charles was even more pop – rock 'n' roll, if you like – but as a jazz pianist he was excellent, and his bulging portfolio of vocal releases was punctuated by occasional all-instrumental albums. He'd also worked with Basie and, on 1959's *Soul Brothers* LP, with Milt Jackson of The Modern Jazz Quartet. Blind and mainlining on heroin, Charles was so worshipped that a British female fan offered him her eyes.

Charles may have agreed with Jimi Hendrix's perspective on jazz – 'a lot of horns and top-speed bass lines. Most of those cats are playing nothing but blues'[5] – reiterating, unknowingly, skiffle scribe Brian Bird: 'Blues, then, may be looked upon as the main content of jazz.'[6] Brian Jones found it convenient to be of the same mind, partly because he had accepted that if he wasn't to be a Cannonball Adderley or Freddie Green in a wider world, he could be distinctive in, ostensibly, a simpler option than jazz. Though he continued to fret guitar behind the toot-tooting of John Keen, Bill Nile *et al* 'he saw it as a crusade to play blues', explained Keen.[3]

Experience of gen-u-ine black American blues by Brian and other UK victims of the same passion had not been limited to mere records. As early as 1944, when in the US army, Howlin' Wolf – as Private Chester Burnett – was stationed in Lincolnshire and, in a fit of exuberance, had done a turn for his GI buddies and civilian drinkers in a village pub. However, elderly Mississippi 'songster' Big Bill Broonzy's London concert in September 1951 has been accepted generally as the British blues movement's sluggish conception – though the previous summer, Josh White (albeit as much a gospel as a blues artist) had appeared for a week as part of a variety presentation at the Chiswick Empire – where both Lonnie Donegan and Alexis Korner wormed their way backstage to pay gushing respects.

If less ebullient a Josh White fan, Chris Barber was as major a catalyst in the development of British blues as Alexis Korner – for, unlike others who merely acted as agents for tours, he financed the conservation of the form. In the teeth of frequent advice to the contrary from the National Jazz Federation, and monetary losses such as that suffered on an hour and a quarter of Muddy Waters in October 1958 at St Pancras Town

Hall and then in the West End at the Federation's own venue, the Marquee, Barber had underwritten visits by many leading US blues – and gospel – artists, including Little Walter, Muddy Waters, Sister Rosetta Tharpe, Roosevelt Sykes and Brownie McGhee's multi-instrumental duo with Sonny Terry, whom Mike Cooper saw at Reading Town Hall as 'special guests' of Chris's New Orleans Jazz Band.

Blues infiltrated Barber's own repertoire, too, sung by either Chris's then-wife Ottilie Patterson, an ex-art teacher from Belfast, or Alexis Korner who, from broadcasting on BFN in Germany, had been Lonnie Donegan's deputy and then his replacement with Barber, having first penned sleeve notes (as 'Alex Korner') for a 1953 EP by Ken Colyer's Jazzmen[7] featuring Donegan and 33-year-old Barber, and supplied appositely toiling grunts on the beat on Ken Colyer-as-skiffler's 78rpm crack at Leadbelly's 'Take This Hammer'.

Korner was probably the first professional British musician to try Muddy Waters' 'I Got My Mojo Working', which became the movement's anthem – though among close seconds were Ma Rainey's 'See See Rider' (recorded by Barber in 1957), 'Hoochie Coochie Man', John Lee Hooker's 'Boom Boom', and 'Baby Please Don't Go', erroneously credited to Ottilie Patterson and augmented by a visiting Sonny Boy Williamson's harmonica. Another contender was Bobby Troupe's '(Get Your Kicks On) Route 66'.[8]

These were heard almost exclusively in the context of a Donegan-length interval spot of maybe four numbers – and Alexis Korner wondered if a show consisting entirely of blues was feasible. With another Barber sideman, mouth organist Cyril Davis, he had in 1957 tried and failed to establish a 'Blues and Barrelhouse' club in a Soho pub, drawing but three customers on what was both the inaugural and final evening. Since then, an unabashed Korner and Davis had been sounding out musicians who might be interested in forming the kingdom's first all-blues outfit. They'd already given it a name: Blues Incorporated.

British press reaction to blues was odd. Reviewing a Muddy Waters recital, Jack Florin of the *Manchester Evening News* wrote, 'Although his singing is authentic and he uses his voice as an instrument for conveying melancholy and dissatisfaction, I cannot class him as a true Blues artist.'[9]

Brian Jones thought otherwise the following year, when he and Richard Hattrell hitchhiked to London to catch Muddy Waters at the Marquee with his Fender Telecaster and regular pianist Otis Spann, plus Chris Barber's drummer and bass player. On this, the first occasion that Brian ever heard a solid-body electric blues guitar in concert, his path became clear. He wandered into the autumn night afterwards, lost in dreams and already half-formed ambition. He was going to teach himself to play like that, and one day either form his own blues group or insinuate his way into whatever existing unit – anywhere in Britain – was closest to one.

4 Halfway To Paradise

'When he moved to London, he still owed me two pounds – which
I never got back.'

– Barry Miles[1]

Brian was to be as captivated by Elmore James as he was by Muddy
Waters. Because the Windy City aggravated his asthma, James was more
reluctant a migrant than Waters after he entered the 'sepia' – as opposed
to the 'popular' and 'country and western' – charts in *Billboard*, the US
music business periodical. His records were obtainable easily enough
outside North America, but Elmore James would always be something
of an acquired taste for most white blues enthusiasts in his trademark
application of prewar bluesman Robert Johnson's rural bottleneck (or
slide) technique to electric guitar. Nevertheless, he struck a chord with
Brian Jones, who, after much hard listening, discovered that James did
not either play in orthodox fashion or use standard tuning.

'He used to play me Robert Johnson and Elmore James records,'
reminisced Pat Andrews, 'and explain how they got their sounds. He
believed they used actual bottle necks to get the slide effect – so he broke
a bottle neck off and tried it. He got the sound, but it was a bit dangerous.
One day, we went round to a number of garages, and Brian found a bit
of pipe cut to fit his finger.'

Slide – or bottleneck – guitar playing is traceable to Hawaiian music
as well as early blues – and not dissimilar to the pedal steel in C&W.
Brian had heard one on a recent hit, 'Sleepwalk', by Santo and Johnny.
Both pedal steel and bottleneck involve exploring the possibilities of
glissandi rather than 'clean' notes, via the careen of strings tuned to an

open chord, and a fret board stroked with a 'slide', usually a glass or metal tube placed on the finger. Lowell George, one of the most renowned exponents in the 1970s, began with the casing of a spark plug. Because it is necessary to heighten the bridge, the frets become only an approximate visual guide on where to find a given note. This means that an ear able to differentiate between pitch variables of at least quarter-tones is essential to accurate bottleneck playing.

With no one to instruct him or even a worthwhile manual available, Brian learned what he could from discs and by trial-and-error after winding his instrument with heavy-gauge strings. Though Elmore James lurked in the shadows as he practised, Brian's slide-playing soon became as distinctive a musical signature as the mark of Zorro via an exactness of phrasing and a ringing, if sometimes stentorian, clarity that was all the more rewarding for its studied restraint.

Yet Brian wasn't sure if an ex-grammar schoolboy from Cheltenham was qualified to play the blues on bottleneck or anything else. His was hardly the Twisted Voice of the Underdog, was it? He didn't risk going to the electric chair for shooting a man in Cheltenham. Memphis rolled off the tongue easier. So did New York, New Orleans, Chicago, Kansas and St Louis. He couldn't get the blues eating fish and chips in a Prestbury Road armchair like you could picking at a 'mess of grits' – whatever that was – in the jailhouse, waking up in an empty bed, turning the key to the highway or looking at the bottom of a whisky glass. Moreover, Brian wasn't blind or crippled. Asthma didn't count as a blues affliction, except if you were Elmore James. Neither was Brian suffering from alcoholism or some sort of drug addiction. Finally, he wasn't black, and, no matter how many men he shot in Memphis, 'Brian Jones' as a blues name didn't have the same ring to it as, say, 'Blind Lemon Jefferson', 'Roosevelt Sykes' or 'John Lee Hooker'.

One day, Brian thought of giving himself the stage alias 'Elmore Lewis' or, less obvious a genuflection to his hero, 'Elmo Lewis', but it remained unspoken while he dealt with a new – or, perhaps, not so new – personal crisis. Pat Andrews, so he confided to Richard Hattrell and then others, was 'up the duff'. Comparatively fresh from school, Pat hadn't associated either her and her boyfriend's activities between the sheets or the cessation of her periods with pregnancy, and she hadn't told him until it was too late for her to do anything other than have the baby – which was due the following autumn.

Pat, nevertheless, wasn't so naive as to imagine a pretty, romantic scene, with Brian proposing on one knee and promising to love her for ever. 'Marriage was never discussed,' she said. 'In any case, at first my parents completely denied that Brian could have anything to do with it, even though he had a track record. My mother was absolutely horrified, and my dad was probably hurt more than anyone because I was his favourite. His hurt was because he thought I would be hurt. He didn't criticise me once.

'Donald, the youngest of my two brothers, was usually as quiet as a mouse, but he'd always been my protector and defender. Brian told me that Donald had gone into the Bar-B-Q coffee bar, and pinned Brian up against the wall, and said something along the lines of "How dare you do this to my sister!", but it's not in any of our family's nature to be physically violent – though my mother once clonked him on the head with her umbrella along the Promenade. She adored this umbrella – one of those pencil-thin ones that were the fashion then – but it dented in the shape of Brian's head. Yet my mother remained fond of Brian. Everyone in the family did.'

The new addition – male – arrived on 23 October 1961. 'Brian was thrilled,' grinned Pat. 'My recollection is of being in the nursing home and seeing this big bouquet of flowers with hands and legs walking towards me. When Brian's cheeky grin peeped from behind it, I asked him how on earth he could afford it. He said he'd sold four of his albums – which I knew meant a great deal to him. Not only that, but he'd bought me a mohair skirt and matching sweater to wear when I left hospital.'

Brian insisted the boy be called Julian after Cannonball Adderley, but from the cradle he was known by his middle name, Mark. The mother's family did not, as yet, put financial pressure on Brian, knowing as they did that here was a man of straw. Music – especially the kind he favoured – wasn't going to make Brian rich. It was seen as a vocational blind alley by the ordinary working man, unless you either taught it or had been born into show business.

Yet, for all the present turmoil – regrettable rather than disastrous – Brian strove to keep a concrete decision about the future at arm's length. At Prestbury Road all he could do was dream and despair, lying fully dressed, head under hands, on the bed where Mark had been conceived. He'd pad over to the window to gaze glumly at the traffic outside. Then, if no one else was in, he might position himself with his guitar in front of the wardrobe mirror and, in a time-honoured ritual of thwarted eroticism, perform to thousands of ecstatic females that only he could see.

He felt no end of a fool, too, when he shook a frustrated fist in the direction of London, which was only maybe three hours away on the train, but might as well have been Saturn. The road he was on was obscure, a dusty, wearisome road that didn't look as if it led anywhere important – but there was always a chance that it might.

You only had to be in the right place at the right time, hadn't you? He'd read in *Melody Maker* that a church hall in Putney had been the scene of a one-night-only blues club the previous September. It encompassed records and what was billed as the 'debut of a fabulous new group, Benny Green's Rhythm And Blues All Stars'.

Brian knew all about Benny. He'd been on tenor sax in Lord Rockingham's XI, the house band on *Oh Boy!*, and functioned now as a music critic who, biting the hand that had fed him, was especially scathing about rock 'n' roll. He was also a BBC radio 'personality' of Steve Race kidney, and one of a self-contained caste with first refusal on virtually all London studio dates.

Brian could imagine that Green's transitory Rhythm And Blues All Stars hadn't been very good. He guessed, too, that Blues Incorporated, which was quorate at last, would be – even if Alexis Korner's principal income came from numerous unbluesy voice-overs for ITV commercials in his BFN announcer's mahogany husk. He and Cyril Davies were also part of the London session crowd with the likes of Benny Green, drummer Andy White from the Vic Lewis Orchestra and Brian Poole And The Tremeloes, signed initially by Decca as a backing vocal group. Poole remembered, 'Cyril was late for a session. He turned up in a full-length raincoat with holes in the pockets, and about ten harmonicas fell out of the hem of it. He asked what key the number was in, and then did a perfect take.'

Alexis, however, was a mediocre and stylistically limited guitarist, but he held his own when he, Cyril, singer Long John Baldry and tenor saxophonist Dick Heckstall-Smith – the nucleus of what would be Blues Incorporated – turned up as part of the package when a London jazz amalgam under the aegis of trumpeter Ken Sims descended on St Luke's Hall one September Thursday in 1961.

Detained by a heavily pregnant Pat, Brian, testy and sweating, was late, catching only the 'I Got My Mojo Working' finale, but he was placated when the Londoners accepted a few after-hours drinks back at Prestbury Road. Whereas fellow tenant Graham Ride, a talented woodwind player, buttonholed Dick Heckstall-Smith, Alexis Korner and an amazing young man talked blues and picked at guitars in the kitchen.

Had Brian ever enjoyed a more interesting conversation? The feeling seemed to be reciprocal, because Jones was the first British bottleneck player Korner had ever heard. Theirs was, therefore, a cordial encounter, but, though Alexis's and Brian's eyes met through the cigarette smoke, neither knew then to what extent their careers would interweave.

Before he left that night, Korner mentioned that he'd be appearing locally again shortly at the Town Hall, in his capacity as featured vocalist with Chris Barber. It'd be great, he said, if Brian, Graham and their pals could get along to that one.

Brian spent the afternoon before squeezing out blackheads, shampooing his hair and polishing his winkle-pickers. He laid out his shirt (with button-down collar), slim-jim tie and the narrow-lapelled Italian suit that he'd collected from the laundry, having promised that he'd have the law on them if it wasn't pressed in time.

The early winter chill hit like a hammer on the way to the Town Hall, but Brian felt infinitely patient, rehearsing mentally what he was going to say to Alexis after the show, and the cool way he'd do so. Civic promoters frowned on 'guest lists' in those days, so it had been the put-upon Pat Andrews who had paid for the tickets when they, together with John Keen and Richard Hattrell, were Korner's wildly applauding claque during his brief solo spot.

Afterwards, and backstage at a Sonny Terry and Brownie McGhee appearance in Cheltenham a few days later, Brian nattered with proud familiarity to Alexis, who was in two minds about whether to counsel him to take his chances in London – where a now fully mobilised Blues Incorporated were searching for premises in which to establish a weekly club – but it was the advice the 19-year-old wished to hear.

Within weeks, Brian's search for like-minded musicians took him halfway there. Alexis put him in touch with an entity in Oxford called Thunder Odin And His Big Secret, fronted by an acne-pitted singing mouth-organist named Paul Pond, and with a repertoire that embraced a wide range of blues forms – particularly Chicago.

Paul had had a similar *idée fixe* to Brian since frequenting Pete Russell's Hot Record Store as a schoolboy in his native Plymouth: 'One day, Pete said to me, "You like blues? Listen to this." He played me this stuff which had a big, hard backbeat, a big chunky piano and a fat bass. "What is this!?" "T-Bone Walker." "This man is a genius!" "Yes," said Pete. "Many people already know this. What's taken you so long?"' One track, "Play On Little Girl", had harmonica.'[2]

This album was added by Paul to those he'd already acquired by the jazz and blues artists Chris Barber and Lonnie Donegan had said they liked in *Melody Maker* interviews. Record sessions evolved into Paul and his chums attempting to reproduce the sounds themselves. By the time he started his arts degree at Oxford, Pond was endeavouring to copy the energetic style of Muddy Waters' sometime harmonica players, Little Walter and Junior Wells: 'I don't know what I sounded like then, but it was Brian Jones who said to me one day, "If you want to sound like Little Walter, then you have to take that C harmonica and play it in the key of G on it." Since then, I've found that to be not exactly true. Lots of harp players play it in the regular key – and that includes Little Walter.

'Brian and I did briefly have a band together. Brian would stop off at Oxford and stay overnight at my place. By this time, I'd been sent down from university. It must have been late 1961 or the beginning of '62. There was always a party going on. If my band was playing one, Brian would often sit in with us.'[2]

An Oxford blues band might have seemed a contradiction in terms, but the word was spreading. 'Bristol, Newcastle and Reading, along with London, were the places for blues in the early 1960s,' noted the late Jo Ann Kelly – who, with Mike Cooper, was to be a cult celebrity during a second wave of British blues in the later 1960s. She continued, 'In Newcastle, there were The Hokum Hotshots and Gordon Smith. In Reading, there was Mike Cooper and a harmonica player, Jerry Kingett. In Bristol, there were Ian A Anderson, Al Jones, The Deep... It seemed to be a city thing on the whole, rather than rural.'[3]

Cheltenham wasn't one of Jo Ann's or anyone else in the know's 'places for blues' – and neither, to Brian's dismay, was Oxford, owing to the transient nature of the Thunder Odin personnel, which precluded anything beyond rehearsal and the recording of a 'grim'[4] tape that they mailed to Alexis Korner – so grim that the recipient didn't mention it when next he, Brian and Paul met.

Pond – who was to adopt the *nom de théâtre* 'PP Jones' and then just plain 'Paul Jones' – was about to seek his fortune in London, and thought it would be a logical move for Brian, too. Yet, as well as the much-increased opportunity to find artistic kinship, a spell outside his usual orbit seemed a fine notion to Brian for other reasons as well.

The gang was breaking up, most of them departing to the world of work, the marriage bed or, in the case of Richard Hattrell, national service as a mechanical engineer in Germany, followed by three years in the part-time Territorial Army, which involved, annually, a fortnight's summer camp plus two weekends in the winter.

Brian didn't envy Richard his dung-coloured uniform and regulation haircut, planed halfway up the skull, but there were dismissed moments when he imagined he would have preferred the orderliness of military life to the close and guilt-inducing smell of soiled nappies around Pat and Mark, the potential complications of further parochial romantic pursuits and his own tight-lipped parents still deluding themselves that they owned his life and that his 'better self' could be reclaimed.

They'd come near to washing their hands of him. He'd drop by now and then, generally if he was trying to cadge money to, say, pay off his rent arrears. If he spent the night, they'd feel like hoteliers. Once, they'd disappeared to Wales for Christmas without telling him, teaching Brian a further lesson by locking the house against his expected reappearance for the supposed festivities. They knew about Pat's baby, of course, but there'd been nowhere like the commotion they'd been with Valerie, no anguished conclave between them and that Andrews family, thank God.

Yet a peace agreement between Brian and his parents seemed to be pending. There was a little less of an 'atmosphere', and a tangible sign of progress was Brian thinking aloud to Lewis and Louise about a steady job, a mortgage, maybe wedding bells. He didn't go so far as to suggest he'd flushed the music nonsense out of his system, but he wanted, so he emphasised, to disengage himself from his frivolous Cheltenham acquaintances like Henry V had Falstaff – and the only way to do so was to leave not only Prestbury Road but the town altogether.

Mr and Mrs Jones weren't born yesterday. There'd been a lightning conversion after Valerie, too. Yet, thrusting aside doubts, they got on with what needed to be done with whatever tools were available. Among these were the science A-levels and a kinder testimonial than either they or their wayward son might have expected from Dr Bell.

Brian went along with whatever would shut them up, as long as it was a means to escape to London. He didn't interrupt when his father droned on about the opportunities in dentistry, maybe, or physiotherapy, and, with hardly a murmur, applied for a course at (God knows why) the London College of Applied Optics, beginning in the New Year. Lewis's reasoning behind this was that, though it wasn't university, if Brian stuck at it he'd be well placed to gain a job with a decent salary – and in a suit rather than overalls. What more could he want?

There was a hint of Brian's hidden agenda less than an hour after the interview, to which he was accompanied by his father. While they were waiting for the train home at Paddington station, Brian decided – on the apparent spur of the moment – that nothing would do, but he had to sample some of the West End jazz clubs. Then he strode off, intending to get up to Lewis knew not what.

What Brian was not intending to do was become an optician – or a dentist, physiotherapist, pedicurist, tree surgeon or any other of his father's suggestions of how to make use of his A-levels. In the first instance, Brian attended to just that modicum of work necessary to prevent expulsion, but, to all intents and purposes, he quit the London College of Applied Optics with indecent haste during a spring term of skipped lectures, overall passive disinterest and an extramural objective with which none of the other students could have identified.

Alexis Korner, however, understood perfectly, and he and wife Bobbie made Brian welcome for tea-and-biscuits in their Bayswater flat. Sometimes, Brian would pop in after he'd sirred and madamed from nine till five thirty at the Civil Service Stores along the Strand. It wasn't exactly show business, but it would do while he bounced ideas off Alexis and searched central London and beyond for prospective members of the blues group that in reveries he imagined would make a living, if not his fortune.

There'd been approaches to Brian already by Ben Palmer, former pianist with Thunder Odin, who'd appealed via the 'Musicians Wanted' section of *Melody Maker* for anyone interested in starting a blues outfit based in Surrey. Among those who replied was guitarist Tom McGuiness, by day an assistant in a Kingston furniture shop. His girlfriend attended the local art school with a certain Eric Clapton. 'All she knew about him', recalled Ben, 'was that he liked playing the guitar.'[2] Ben, Eric, Tom and others who'd responded to the advertisement rehearsed at a pub in Guildford, but didn't get much further than giving the affiliation a name, The Roosters.

With no financial gain in mind beyond beer and petrol money, their lack of leadership – as well as a glaring absence of a bass player – made inevitable their disintegration within six months. 'At the time, there weren't many people who wanted to play in a rhythm-and-blues band,' added McGuiness. 'You really felt as if it was a branch of Freemasonry.'

Possibly because it would have been one guitarist too many, Brian chose not to involve himself with The Roosters. Besides, the rearing up of family commitments had put a temporary tin lid on any messing about of any sort. Since opting out of Applied Optics, he'd established a pattern of doing a runner whenever landlords pressed for perhaps weeks of unpaid rent. However, he'd settled in a bedsit along a forlorn sideroad a stone's throw from Hampstead Cemetery, when an enraged Pat had turned up suddenly, pushing Mark's pram with one hand and clasping a too-full suitcase in the other.

She had learned that Brian had been corresponding with another Cheltenham girl, whom he'd invited to London for a weekend. 'He was not the faithful kind, but I think that was due to lack of confidence,' groaned Pat, 'but, there and then, I cashed my maternity benefit and bought a ticket for the London coach, which left at three in the morning. I knew my parents would go out that evening – and, as soon as they did, I packed as much as I could (mainly Mark's stuff), left a note and headed for a friend's, where I stayed until half past two. Then she and her husband accompanied me to the coach station. Luckily, the coach was in early. As it prepared to leave, I saw policemen. I had to slide down in the seat so they wouldn't see me.

'I got to Victoria at half past seven with seven shillings [35p/55c] and a Hampstead address in my pocket. As soon as I got to Brian's, I wrote home to say I was all right. Brian posted it in the Strand so that no one could trace me.'

The Strand wasn't to be the location of Brian's place of work for much longer. For fractional more money and far less travel, he'd be selling carpets and then electrical goods in Whiteley's, a department store just round the corner from the Korners, and one stop on London's internal railway from Notting Hill where, because the Hampstead bedsit was designed for one, Brian had found an adequate flat after Mark had to be placed in foster care for several weeks and Pat found a job in a laundry.

Now that matters were on a relatively even keel, Brian was able to focus once more on his main purpose in moving to London. He and Paul Jones had already come forth from the throng gathered at the G Club, where Blues Incorporated were now resident. It was in a basement between a teashop and a jeweller's along Ealing Broadway, and its opening at 7:30pm on St Patrick's Day 1962 had been heralded in a *Melody Maker* notice with a captioned endorsement from Chris Barber that wished 'the first R&B club [*sic*] in the country every possible success'.[5]

Unlike the ill-fated Blues and Barrelhouse night five years earlier and the effort centred on Benny Green, the G Club had been patronised immediately by fire regulation-breaking zealots from London, Middlesex, Surrey and further, all as earnestly devoted to blues as other cliques were to yachting, numismatics, animal welfare and Freemasonry. Most of them were students, weekend dropouts or middle-class bohemians who might have 'dressed down' for the occasion – in frayed jeans, Jesus sandals, holey pullover, carefully tousled hair and CND badge – while *Jimmy Reed At Carnegie Hall* or the plaintive debut album by Bob Dylan warmed up the Dansette. Alternatively, if in highbrow mood, they'd dry their hair to Coltrane, Parker or Adderley.

Some listeners were players themselves who were responsible for a fair number of musical assassinations, having got up from the audience to thrash guitars and holler gutbucket exorcisms with the loose collective presided over by Korner and Cyril Davis. Among these was a nervous Economics student called Mick Jagger who, with another future Rolling Stone, drummer Charlie Watts, was to be – like Long John Baldry was already – a semi-permanent member of Blues Incorporated.

'Brian and I were just among the many young hopefuls,' laughed Paul Jones, 'and we would stand as close as we could to the stage because Alexis was very generous, and would let the youngsters up to play.'[2] The Jones boys' turn had come on 7 April 1962, when Paul sang Elmore James's *magnum opus* 'Dust My Broom' – as 'Dust My Blues' – from behind huge sunglasses, backed by a seated and smartly dressed Brian's unprecedented bottleneck.

They ended to a thunderous cheer. 'Paul Jones sang well, but Brian was absolutely brilliant,' gasped Dick Taylor, a friend of Mick Jagger and another geezer there that night, Keith Richards.

5 Bachelor Boy

'Suppose we failed to get anywhere – would it matter? At least we'd have tried, and we would have nothing to regret in later life, never knowing how good we could have been.'

– Brian Jones[1]

Almost three-quarters of Brian Jones's life was over when, following that transfixing 'Dust My Blues', Dick Taylor, Mick Jagger, Keith Richards and the rest of an entourage from where London bleeds into Kent threaded across the G Club to flock round him like friendly if over-attentive wolfhounds. Most round-eyed of all was the usually reticent Richards, combining delighted exclamation and appearing nonchalantly informed about Elmo-Brian's methodology. 'Brian used open G tuning,' exemplified Taylor, 'which Keith was aware of, but didn't use himself until at least 1968.'

This was as momentous an opening encounter as that of John Lennon and Paul McCartney at a church fête in 1957. It was Keith, Dick – both guitarists – and Mick's third visit to the G Club, and Brian's final performance with Paul Jones, who was to mark time – as 'Paul Petersen' – belting out assembly-line pop with Slough's Gordon Reece And The Adelphians, prior to enrolment in what was to become Manfred Mann. The line-up was to also include Tom McGuiness – though, not long after the sundering of The Roosters in early 1963, he and Eric Clapton made up half of The Engineers, who backed Casey Jones, a vocalist whose Liverpool accent was a crucial bartering tool for a one-shot single for EMI.

Merseybeat was, however, distant thunder when, following his brief but acclaimed liaison with Paul Jones, Brian short-listed potential candidates for a group with fixed personnel rather than the constant flux of Blues Incorporated's open-ended evenings of blues structures so stylised that, while playing them, you could wonder if you'd remembered to collect the eiderdowns from the dry-cleaners. The Ealing honeymoon had been over quickly. 'We reckoned Alexis Korner's band was fantastic the first week,' summarised Dick Taylor, 'quite good the second, but by the third week, we thought it was really a bit off.'

For some it was less to do with the Sound than the Look. You could sing like a nightingale or make a guitar talk, but if you suffered from middle age, obesity or baldness, you'd never get more than a cult following. Though neither gave a damn about a teenage public's feelings about what they were doing, who would scream over portly, baggy-trousered Cyril, sweating over his mouth organ, or moustached Alexis, old enough to be anyone's dad?

'I saw Jagger with them,' remembered Don Craine, then a student at Acton Hotel and Catering College, 'but it was a young guy sitting in with a bunch of old jazzers – though they were probably only in their 30s at most. Blues Incorporated's take on R&B didn't impress me, and couldn't see a future for it outside the jazz clubs. It certainly wasn't going to make it with the kids.'

While there were never-to-be-repeated tangents like the Jones and Jones duo, to Craine, Dick Taylor and other younger members of the G Club, it was as if serious British blues wasn't going to be played in any other way or by any other musicians than the self-contained phalanx in and around Blues Incorporated. Too many of those always onstage were, indeed, hardened jazzers. There was still an aura of the trad dad about Alexis and Cyril, while drummer Ginger Baker had served Acker Bilk and Terry Lightfoot. Graham Bond had blown 'modern' alto sax with Don Rendell, and Jack Bruce had been with The Scottsville Jazzmen before trading in his double bass for a Fender electric. With Dick Heckstall-Smith, Bond and Bruce had played together in the mainstream Johnny Burch Octet.

Cracks were appearing within Blues Incorporated, too. By the time its debut LP, *R&B From The Marquee*[2] – where Korner had negotiated a Thursday-night residency – was issued in autumn 1962, The Graham Bond Organisation, plotted as a tighter, jazzier take on Blues Incorporated,

– was a twinkle in the eyes of Bond, Baker, Bruce and Heckstall-Smith, and Cyril Davies was mithering about his preference for a narrower, Chicago-style interpretation of the music rather than Korner's 'everything from Louis Jordan to Martha and the Vandellas'.[3]

It wasn't all smiles between Blues Incorporated and Long John Baldry, either so, with his ear to the ground, Brian was on Baldry's case with the promptness of a vulture. However, the blond giant was being courted more intensely by Davies, who intended to found a suitably purist club in Harrow-on-the-Hill with himself leading a house band, The All-Stars. Brian also rubbed his chin over Tony McPhee and Peter Cruikshank, respectively a guitarist and bass player, who'd been on the periphery of those surrounding Brian and Paul after their G Club triumph. Tony and Peter, however, had been charged with finding a drummer for a trio, The Groundhogs, to accompany John Lee Hooker on a forthcoming tour of Europe.

Jones next hovered round guitarists Geoff Bradford and Brian Knight, each old enough to have played at the ill-fated Blues and Barrelhouse Club, but now members of Blues By Six with Charlie Watts and saxophonist Art Themen. 'We were doing the interval gig for Blues Incorporated at the old Marquee,' recalled Geoff, 'when I was approached by a small, lisping person who turned out to be Brian Jones – who struck me as a most peculiar person to be playing slide guitar. He asked if I was interested in joining a blues band. Always ready for a blow, I agreed.'[4]

Commuting virtually every Saturday from Reading to Ealing, Mike Cooper, too, 'had a conversation with Brian Jones about the group he wanted to form. It sounded good to me.' It didn't occur to Brian to approach the G Club's Kentish contingent yet, but they were on the spot anyway when he booked consecutive midweek afternoons in the functions room of Soho's Bricklayers' Arms, and advertised – three lines unboxed – in *Jazz News*, a London periodical bought mainly for its venue information and irregular features such as a column by Manfred Mann.

Brian held the door open first of all for Ian Stewart, an unlikely looking cove with a desk-bound shipping clerk's short haircut, lederhosened bicycle-club thighs and the beefy mitts with which he pounded a surprisingly agreeable boogie-woogie on the worn-out pub piano. Before the week was out, Keith Richards and Dick Taylor, both studying at Sidcup Art College – plus the slightly more illustrious bluesman, Mick Jagger – were among other candidates, which also included 'a drummer with only half a kit', noticed Geoff Bradford,[4] who, with Brian Knight, was judged by Stewart and Jones to be head and shoulders above Richards and Taylor as more 'authentic' blues instrumentalists – and certainly far better than Alan Etherington and Bob Beckwith, who mucked about on guitars with Dick and Keith back in northwest Kent in not so much a group as a blues appreciation society. Whatever it was, it had hitherto given no performance in public.

The various factions were at loggerheads almost immediately. 'Geoff Bradford and Brian Knight thought Keith was too rock 'n' roll,' remembered Dick Taylor, 'and stomped off in a purist huff. The bass player, whoever he was, went with the general stampede as well.'

To the discerning Mike Cooper, too, 'when Mick and Keith turned up, suddenly it all sounded too commercial. In retrospect, I also perhaps didn't like Jagger and Richards. It was nothing to do with them really. I was always very antisocial with certain "up-front" personality types, and those two were – or at least Mick was. I didn't like Chuck Berry then, either, and I couldn't see a group with them in it going in a way that would lead down a jazz-R&B road.'

After more than a month of further try-outs at the Bricklayers' Arms and other licensed premises, auditions mutated into rehearsals, and antagonistic youths milling around whittled down to a group containing Jones, Stewart, Jagger, Richards – and Taylor, who'd been induced by Brian to invest £25 ($40) in an Emperor bass guitar.

The amenable Taylor's reflections on Jones's conduct and attitude then are useful: 'Brian regarded himself as leader because he'd invited Mick, Keith and I to join – whereas we thought it was a logical development of what we'd been doing with Robert Beckwith and Alan Etherington. It was really a hybrid of that and Brian's band – which was on the way to being fully formed by him and Ian Stewart.

'They liked the idea of having Mick as a singer. He'd seen his potential at the Ealing Club, and thought he could transform their band – and wherever Mick went, Keith came too – and they invited me along as well. Brian was very complimentary about my bass playing – though when I first started learning, I didn't have many problems because it was just a case of figuring out a few riffs through listening to what seemed to be the bass lines on disc. They were often more a presence than a sound on domestic record players in those days.

'Depending on where was free, we convened either at the Bricklayers', the White Bear behind Leicester Square or the Wetherby Arms in King's Road. Brian was sometimes late because he was working at Whiteley's. He seemed more of a grown-up than us, but he was capable of being pretty damned moody, mostly about how things were going with the group. He didn't want us necessarily to be rich and famous then, but he did want us to find work. I think he was introverted and maybe insecure, but, although he'd despair and get out of his head a bit, he had an acute sense of humour in those days, a very amusing person. In the beginning, everyone was great mates, and we used to have lots of laughs.'

There had been, for instance, amusement rather than annoyance when rehearsals at the White Bear ceased after the landlord caught Jones clambering over the unattended bar in the upstairs room to steal cartons of cigarettes. The discord, intrigues and general unpleasantnesses that make pop groups what they are did not become overt until it was discovered much later that Brian had been taking 'agency commissions' from the meagre payments the group received for the intermittent engagements that disrupted the working week, college timetables and recreational sloth during the latter half of 1962.

The first had been at the Marquee – then in Oxford Street – on 12 July, deputising with a stand-in drummer for a streamlined Blues Incorporated, who'd been booked for the BBC Light Programme's *Jazz Club* that evening. The BBC was prepared to pay only for five musicians, necessitating such cost-cutting expedients as Korner doubling on lead vocals, and dispensing with the services of Long John Baldry, who was keeping his options open by singing with both Blues Incorporated and the nascent Cyril Davis All-Stars.

Mick Jagger was out of the frame, too, but he, like everyone else, regarded the *Jazz Club* slot as a breakthrough for the British blues movement (or 'rhythm and blues', as it was becoming) in general rather than just for Alexis *et al*. Therefore, to keep the light burning, Long John Baldry and an ad hoc ensemble, The Hoochie Coochie Men, with Geoff Bradford on lead guitar, were to be the main attraction that Thursday, and Brian Jones was asked by Korner if his untried group could fill the intermission spot.

A-twitter with excitement, the lads' non-stop preparation for their concert debut included someone – and all fingers point to Brian – coming up with a corporate nomenclature to go with publicity relating to that particularly booking. 'The Rollin' Stones' – or, to be precise, 'Brian Jones & Mick Jagger & The Rollin' Stones' – would do for now, he assured Ian Stewart, who was especially disgruntled with the name. They could alter it later.

Its precedents were mixed. On one hand, 'Rollin' Stone Blues' was the title of the first single by Muddy Waters to be issued in Britain (a 78, in 1953) – and 'rollin' stone' was a throwaway phrase in another Waters number. Into the bargain, there'd been a 1957 Lonnie Donegan B-side, 'I'm Just A Rollin' Stone'.

Conversely, The Rolling Stones were a cartoon circus family[5] in a pre-teen comic called *Robin*. It was also the name of a group then operational in Bristol, just as there was another one called The Who from Sheffield, as well as The Zombies over in Bath, Dave Dee And His Deemen in the West Midlands and Them, pride of Liphook.

Just as far too many would profess to have been at Belfast's Club Rado for the more illustrious Them, or at the Cavern for The Beatles or to have seen The Sex Pistols' early fiascos, so there would be a profound lack of retrospective honesty about the first manifestation of The Rolling Stones. Hundreds more than can actually have been there were to conjure memories of that maiden appearance at the Marquee. Some biographers have portrayed it erroneously as an ignition point for extreme reaction. Yet, while it didn't provoke a riot, there was a polarisation of opinion.

'The audience was like Christianity versus Islam,' recalled Dick Taylor. 'The scene was dominated by trad jazz – so you can imagine what it was like when a bunch of amateur blues players stepped up. We were the wrong colour to play the blues. We did Muddy Waters, Jimmy Reed. It wasn't wall-to-wall Chuck Berry by any means, but neither was it the stuff Blues Incorporated did.'

It might not have appealed to everyone, but the overall feeling, as the neon twilight struck the departing music lovers, was that the support act had provided stimulating entertainment. Their unbottled exuberance – just enough then not to upset the majority of conservative palates – was certainly a key to further recitals at the Marquee before the year was out, as well as sessions at the G Club.

If not to the same degree as Blues Incorporated, there was clearer attention paid to instrumental prowess than there would be when the beat boom placed a firmer emphasis on vocals. The interaction between Jones and Richards was becoming compulsively exquisite. From the beginning, the concept of one cementing the other's runs with subordinate chord-slashing hadn't been a consideration as, over Taylor's low throb, the two learned to anticipate and attend to each other's idiosyncrasies and clichés. 'Brian and Keith used to swap roles around in a way,' observed Dick. 'Both playing lead bits in normal tuning. Brian was probably at the height of his powers then, playing that blues stuff.'

Wistfully, Dick – as dexterous on a six-string fret board as either Jones or Richards – plucked the prescribed simple riffs on his new Emperor as lead and rhythm guitars merged in interlocking harmony. 'I got fed up playing bass rather than guitar.' With a scholarship at the Central College of Art beckoning for September, he was beset, too, with more pragmatic doubts about continuing as a Rolling Stone. The notion of making a living in show business generally, let alone as an R&B musician, was taken seriously by few arty bohemians, and Taylor balked when Jones suggested the Stones go professional. 'Brian was sorry to see me go,' said Dick, 'and we remained good friends.'

As long as it didn't interfere with college, Taylor agreed to help out until a replacement was procured – as did Ricky Fenson from the Cyril Davies All-Stars. Dick's resignation might have presented an opportunity to change the name, but, as no one other than Ian objected much, the group remained The Rollin', or Rolling, Stones. The 'g' came and went and eventually stayed forever – though, as 1963 crept nearer, the future held little outside the orbit of specified metropolitan blues nights, albeit one growing in impetus and cohesion.

Greater London was soon to boast venues in L'Auberge, the Craw Daddy, Sandover Hall, Eel Pie Island hotel and the Crown – all dotted round Richmond, Kingston and Twickenham. As well as the Marquee, soon to move to Wardour Street, among those in the inner city was the Flamingo, also along Wardour Street, the Booker T Club within Shoreditch Town Hall, South Kensington's Crypt Youth Club, as well as the 100 Club, Ken Colyer's Studio 51 and other metropolitan jazz hangouts that had capitulated to new guidelines that would allow pop groups to defile their stages.

Not so precious were places like Putney's St Mary's Hall – location of Benny Green's 1961 bash – and The Red Lion in Sutton, which second-billed the Stones to parochial heroes Ricky Tyrell And His Presidents for successive Friday evenings. 'Music was just music in 1962 and 1963,' explained Brian Poole. 'Any given club might have The Tremeloes and me one night, a trad band the next and Blues Incorporated the night after that. We all appeared on the same nights sometimes.'

The Stones couldn't be too choosy about offers of work, but Brian Jones was once able to gazump the promoter of L'Auberge into paying £12.10s ($21) rather than the £10 ($17) originally agreed. This was divided up as £2 ($3) per man, with the extra ten shillings (50p/80c) added – without the others' knowledge – to Brian's share, and, to be fair, it had been him ringing from a payphone that had secured the booking.

The most willing to picket on the group's behalf, Jones would also lay on a silver-tongued guile with a metaphorical trowel when negotiating with this quizzical pub landlord or that uninterested social secretary. Introducing himself as 'manager', he would weigh every word of his supplicatory letters and calls, made either from a call box or on a telephone at Whiteley's while glancing over his shoulder for nosier members of staff and doing something 'normal' whenever one hoved into view.

They had good cause to be nosy because, as well as making illicit use of the phone for Stones business, Jones was thieving small items of stock and what was, cumulatively, a huge amount of cash from the till. He wasn't a particularly competent sales assistant either, as the receipts swam before budgerigar eyes – because the previous evening, so his superiors gathered from the grapevine, he'd got to bed as the graveyard hours chimed, after making a row at some Teddy Boys' gala or other. He was the one seen sometimes slouching despondently from tube train to work, screwing himself up to go in.

Now and then, he'd dip into a surreptitious pocket for a black or blueish capsule. How else could he cope? Even before he'd left Cheltenham, he had been aware of 'Black Bombers', purple hearts and other outlawed pep pills. A cloak-and-dagger supply could be obtained with ease in London, what with the Government's net-closing Bill 'to penalise the possession and restrict the import of drugs of certain kinds' over a year away. It was no hanging matter, then, if you were caught anyway. As late as October 1964, the *Hampstead And Highgate Express* reported that a Robert James Moir got away with a conditional discharge for being found with not mere pills, but 30g each of cocaine and heroin.[6]

Snatched sleep and a mixture of amphetamines and last night's lingering alcohol intake often rendered Brian Jones hardly able to think straight at Whiteley's. Not permitted to take off his suit jacket, even in summer, he'd muddle through the day on automatic, staying just a few degrees short of open insolence to any customer pausing at his counter. Otherwise, Brian let his body relax and mind go numb with accumulated fatigue, chemical confusion and the spirit-crushing listlessness of the totally bored.

It was a combination of his double life burning the candle to the middle and instances of his petty-cash pilferings coming home to roost that brought Brian to a glass-doored office where the store manager tapped a pencil on a desktop. He was flanked by two security officers as witnesses for the prosecution. It all but came to court, too, but via Brian's application of that lip-trembling pathos that some find endearing and a plausible tale about marital breakdown, it was decided not to call the police, just rid the firm of the wretched fellow forthwith.

Once again, he was out of the soup, but there was now no money to cover his clothes, his records, his guitar strings, his mouth organs, his cigarettes, his beer, his pills – and for keeping girlfriend and baby in the manner to which they'd become accustomed. A handy peg on which to hang his frustrations, Pat had long seen some sort of crunch coming as a culmination of an age of interminable hours of cliff-hanging silences and the same arguments coming up over and over again, building from an irritated trace of vapour on the horizon to a crockery-smashing Wagnerian thunderstorm.

In the Notting Hill square where Mark was picking up a local accent, an evening of noisome home truths would end in an abrupt and inexplicably tearful reconciliation, but Pat and Brian were no longer infatuated teenagers, holding hands around Cheltenham. Now nearly all such pretty fondnesses had gone. Had he read Nietzsche in 1962, Brian, the only Stone with a family to support, might have stumbled upon and agreed with the German philosopher of irrationalism's personal credo – that domesticity is incompatible with a life of constant creativity. For him and Pat, therefore, there had never been much hope.

Not peculiar to Brian alone was a dual code of morality whereby he could mess around with other girls but wouldn't stomach any infidelities from Pat. In London as it was in Cheltenham, he was being 'talked of' with other women again and again, and Pat's generalised suspicion often turned into fact, most conclusively when, 'I went to Sheffield for a week with the girl from the flat downstairs – to stay with her parents. When I got back, Keith Richards' girlfriend was no longer his girlfriend, but she still hung around the Stones. She came up to me crying, and I said, "What's up? Is it Keith?" She told me that she'd gone round to our flat and found Brian there, and they'd ended up together. This was taking advantage of a young, vulnerable girl, so I told him, "I can't handle that. I can take all the others, but I can't take the betrayal of a friendship." I left Brian in the late summer of 1962 because of that, and because he was very jealous, extremely moody. He had a lot on his plate, trying to fulfil his dream.'

Already, Ian Stewart considered Brian to be 'a very weak and easily-led character',[7] and Pat may have felt the same long before. Certainly, she could see through the histrionics and self-flagellations that came after accumulated evidence meant that he had no choice but to splutter out his latest amatory escapade, blaming it and the others on his strait-laced parents and their symbolic castrations for the sake of propriety.

It was, perhaps, an emotional release for both sides when the Notting Hill family split in two. However, without Pat's wage from the laundry, Brian was soon being trailed by an irate rent collector. By autumn, room had been made for him, too, in a poky two-room flat about to be occupied by Mick and Keith. They were soon to bring in a fourth tenant, James Phelge, a printer by trade. Like Barry Miles, he was to be addressed by his surname. Phelge was, said Brian, doing them a favour. They were struggling with the rent, and it wouldn't be such a worry now they knew they had to scrape up less of it.

If handy for the Wetherby Arms – now the principal place to rehearse – the full horror of 102 Edith Grove reared up during Brian's first night there. He jerked in and out of an uneasy doze, waking up shivering to open-mouthed snores. As daybreak pierced the sock-smelling gloom, he perceived bare light bulbs coated with dust, damp plaster which fell at a touch from mildewed walls and the frowsiness of duffel bags for pillows, coats for supplementary blankets, a frayed sofa, a cigarette-holed tablecloth, screwed-up fish-and-chip paper in the fireplace and someone on their way to the toilet used by everyone in the building.

All this was rather unsettling for a lad from Hatherley Road, Cheltenham, where the sugar was in a bowl, not the packet; the milk in a jar, not the bottle and the cups – not mugs – unchipped on non-plastic saucers. Number 102 became even more loathsome when the seasons turned from moist gold to chill marble. Windows iced up and goose flesh rose in a particularly cheerless winter of low temperatures, seething east winds and snow on snow still on the ground at the end of March.

Was the adventure over? Within hours, Brian could be back in Ravenswood, making short work of the meal prepared for him by Mum. Then he might get lost in a cowboy film on television prior to lowering himself into the hot, scented water of the aqua-coloured bath before going to sleep in his own little room again. For all the 'I told you so' recriminations, the whey-faced disappointment about him throwing in the towel at the College of Applied Optics and the winkling out about what he'd been doing since, it wasn't as uninviting a prospect as it may have seemed a few months earlier.

Yet Brian Jones was resilient. The kismet supercool he'd displayed at the G Club during his famous 'Dust My Blues' remained intact for the time being to Mick and the instinctively indolent Keith – for whom Brian was 'a little bundle of energy'.[8] On days when every waterpipe in Edith Grove was frozen, he'd still emerge from the blistered front door, washed, shaved, shampooed, booted and suited for another round of pavement-tramping to venues that might be coaxed into hiring Brian and his fabulous Rolling Stones.

Nevertheless, during the first months of his sojourn at Edith Grove, he would vanish for maybe half a week at a stretch to attend to matters connected with either Pat and Mark, or some new *affaire de coeur*. He was drifting further and further away from paternal responsibilities, and the decidedly non-complaisant mother of his child no longer clung onto any remote belief that he was worth keeping. His compartmentalised life and his lengthening absences nurtured self-reliance in Pat, who, as far as was feasible, was burning her boats and instigating a new beginning.

Yet she wasn't able to dislike Brian, and was supportive of his commendable efforts to lift the Stones off the ground. 'He put in all the hard work,' she affirmed, 'wrote the letters, found the money, signed the contracts. Mick and Keith did absolutely zilch apart from turning up and performing. Everything else was left to Brian.'

A later girlfriend, Anita Pallenberg, agreed that, 'Brian was the one who did the hustling, getting the band together and believing in it – unlike Mick, who couldn't make his mind up whether he wanted to be an accountant. Instead of appreciating what he did, they resented it.'[9]

Actually, Jagger had contemplated pursuing not accountancy, but journalism. Like Dick Taylor, Mick and Keith might not have been that disappointed if the group had fallen apart, sullen as they often were when, after days of inactivity, Brian, raring to go, steered them from the fug of the flat into the midwinter cold, lugging amplifiers and guitars, for a jolting journey to the other side of London, where they were going to be paid in loose change for taking the stage in front of a small audience with only the vaguest notion about the music they had come to hear. As

Brian hadn't yet found a permanent drummer, one had been hooked from a TV meal, and would be marinating the air with curses as he shambled onto the boards.

After the anticipated catcalls and desultory clapping from the scattered horde before them, The Rolling Stones piled into the opening number at twice the speed at which it had been rehearsed, capsizing Mick's vocal. Brian brazened it out, daring the riff-raff to boo. Paradoxically, he'd be barely suppressing an urge to laugh out loud at this antithesis of pop and fame.

Afterwards, Richards and Jagger's shiftless malcontentment often distorted to guffawing, as Jones would be harassed with enough minor problems to start World War III: 'Iris says I'm to be home by eleven. Can you sort out a lift?' 'Oi, Hank Marvin! If you don't get this electrical junk out of here in ten minutes, I'm locking up.' 'Dick's bass is being repaired, and Jack won't lend him his for the gig at Sandover Hall.' Pause. 'What are you going to do about getting Dick a bass then, Brian?'

With Dick Taylor's – and Ricky Fenson's – waning availability, the situation regarding a bass player had become so desperate that Brian cajoled his old Cheltenham pal, Richard Hattrell, both to move into 102 Edith Grove and to take rudimentary lessons, on a borrowed instrument, from Jack Bruce. Three sessions at the Hampstead flat he shared with Graham Bond were sufficient for Bruce to report to Jones that the Stones were barking up the wrong tree with Richard.

Hattrell was, however, willing to be pushed in whatever direction fate – and Brian – ordained. Someone at Edith Grove uttered the phrase 'road manager'. Richard's chief qualification for this post was that he didn't mind being unpaid and unrecompensed, buoyed as he was by a lump sum for recent Territorial Army stints.

Physically, there wasn't much for Richard to do, as the equipment was portable enough to be go via public transport. 'We used to take the instruments and amplifiers on the bus,' said Richard. 'When it stopped at a T-junction or slowed down, we'd avoid the fare by jumping off.' It hadn't occurred to Richard who was going to pay whenever this wasn't possible, but he quickly got the message – and having to shell out for seven came a bit pricey, especially as, so he lamented, 'we were all struggling to survive at Edith Grove. Well, Brian and I were. Mick and Keith were getting money and food from their parents, while I was on national assistance – which was peanuts. Once, I went to sign on, and the lady there took pity on me and gave me some money from her own purse. My health was cracking up, and it was inevitable, I suppose, that I'd eventually go back to Cheltenham. My father got me a job in a country club.'

By then, Ian Stewart had gained access to a van – and the Stones a full-time bass guitarist in Bill Wyman, a friend of Tony Chapman, one of the transient drummers. Indeed, it was through Jones supplicating Chapman that Bill had been lending his instrument every so often to Dick Taylor and then Richard Hattrell.

The group had also poached Charlie Watts from Blues By Six. Both he and Wyman recognised that, while Mick Jagger hogged the central microphone, Brian Jones was the one who mapped out musical direction with, so they understood, the same all-powerful hold over the rest as drummer Dave Clark had over his Dave Clark Five, who then ruled Tottenham Royal Ballroom as surely as The Beatles did the Cavern. 'Brian was by far the most knowledgable about what we were playing,' averred Bill. 'He was the business manager too in those formative days.'[10]

Thanks in great part to Brian's machinations, the Stones headlined at the Marquee on 10 January 1963, and the following three Thursdays. While a capacity audience couldn't yet be taken for granted – far from it – they were shortly to hit their stride as one of the capital's six most active R&B outfits. The others were Blues By Six, The Wes Minster Five (house band at the Flamingo), those led by Cyril Davies and Alexis Korner and, although they planted feet as heavily in jazz as blues, Dave Hunt's Rhythm & Blues Band.

Trombonist Hunt had been sniffy about R&B in *Jazz News* in a telling sentence: 'It's what the rockers call jazz, and the jazzmen call rock 'n' roll.'[11] He also denigrated the Stones as 'a glorified skiffle group',[12] and was, therefore, disconcerted when they took over his residency at the Craw Daddy in Richmond in late January.

'The young Brian Jones was always bending my ear,' grinned promoter Georgio Gomelsky. 'He'd say with his lisp, "You mutht help uth. We have the betht blueth band in the land." So when Hunt hoofed it, I called Ian Stewart at his work – that's how you contacted the Stones then – and asked if they wanted a residency on Sunday nights. Of course they did. The first night, three people came.' [13]

6 Go Away Little Girl

'It wasn't until much later that you realised you were involved in
the start of such a vast thing that swept world-wide.'

– Jane Relf [1]

Jane Relf was among the multitudes that grew weekly from the mere
handful at the Stones' first Sunday night at the Craw Daddy. Her initial
impression was that 'they were quite good, but I didn't like Mick Jagger
because he used to show off – but, soon, it really was an amazing night
out. It was a regular thing to go down and watch the Stones: queueing
for hours to get in, then you just couldn't move in there, bodies just
squashed together. The Shake came in then. It sort of evolved because
people couldn't move. You used to just stand there and just, well, shake…' [2]

Descending on the Craw Daddy in droves were 'youths' and, half a
class up, 'young adults', whose liberal-minded parents might collect them
afterwards in estate cars. Ever-tighter clusters of girls in fishnet, suede
and leather would block the view for the dismayed R&B enthusiast who
recalled the dodgy Blues Incorporated offshoot that had supported Long
John Baldry at the Marquee only a few months earlier. Even in the
hallowed G Club, the first screams had already reverberated for Mick –
and Brian, who now sported less an Adam Faith razor-cut than a then-
shocking exaggeration of a Beatle moptop.

A kind of committed gaiety from an increasingly more uproarious
crowd had lent an inspirational framework to performances that covered
a waterfront from country blues and antique 'Down The Road Apiece'
to the latest from Chuck Berry. In between lay works by Elmore James,
Muddy Waters, Jimmy Reed, Rufus Thomas and Bo Diddley (on whom

the Stones leaned as heavily as they did Berry), and irresistible concessions to the rock 'n' roll end of US mainstream pop. There was even a bit of Johnny Cash in there as well.

Kicking off to thunderous huzzahs, a galvanising squiggle of guitar might plunge the Stones into Chuck's 'Back In The USA' – or possibly his 'Roll Over Beethoven' or 'Beautiful Delilah'. The spooning out of a just-sufficiently-ramshackle lucidity continues as Jones, Wyman, Watts and Richards advance with the grace of fencing masters on 'Hoochie Coochie Man', in which a suspensory hissing high-hat beneath the stop-start five-note riff, played over and over again, stokes the prickly heat to a simmer for Jagger's 'Well, the gypsy woman told my mama' entry, and boils over just as the chord rises finally to a shuffling subdominant and a tension-breaking first chorus.

Then Brian abandons guitar, to emote on recently mastered harmonica the exquisite dirge that is 'Soon Forgotten' from *Muddy Waters At Newport*. Next, he's wielding maracas like a man possessed on a bravura 'Baby What's Wrong' and is back on guitar for an audience-participation number – its title lost in the mists of time – that involves bawling 'five-ten-fifteen-twenty…'

Riding roughshod over tempo refinements, complicated dynamic shifts or, indeed, anything that needed too much thought, a few verse–chorus transitions were cluttered, and certain numbers a fraction too bombastic – but so what? Casually strewn errors were brushed aside like matchsticks as Brian conducted by instinct and eye contact with the jigging onlookers willing him and the others on – worrying when they flagged, cheering when they rallied and glowing when, by the time the Stones resolved into the finale (maybe 'Diddley Daddy', 'Pretty Thing' 'Ride 'Em On Down' or 'Let It Rock'), they'd long been home and dry.

The Stones' casually cataclasymic effect at the Craw Daddy was food for thought among the frayed jeans, CND badges and beatnik beards towards the back, some awaiting destinies as Yardbirds, Kinks or Pretty Things – all groups that would enter the charts within a year. Running in the same pack, The Downliners Sect's career trajectory would be more typical of countless other combos in and around Teddington Lock that owed much to the Stones.

The Sect were traceable to a late 1950's Twickenham unit trading as just plain 'Downliners', treading warily amidst official disapproval of guitars-bass-drums rock 'n' roll at Gunnersbury Grammar School, and operating simultaneously in more blatantly pop mode as Geronimo And The Apaches. When appearing at the 2I's early in 1962, they'd been joined on stage by Casey Jones. Afterwards, he suggested an excursion to an all-nighter at the Flamingo, presided over by Earl Watson And The Blue Flames,[3] and Zoot Money's Big Roll Band.

The Flamingo had worked up a clientele of prototype mods, mostly male blue-collar or low-ranking office workers by day, who recognised each other by their clean, short-haired pseudo-suaveness and whim-conscious dress sense at odds with the aggressively untidy middle-class bohemians heading, so they informed Don Craine, the Sect's singing guitarist, for darkest Ealing.

When seeking further musical recreation, Don began alternating between central and outer London, the Flamingo and the G Club, until 'late in 1962, when a friend recommended that I see this group playing the Station Hotel in Richmond. It turned out to be the Stones. Within a couple of songs, I experienced a road-to-Damascus moment. I thought, "That's it! This is what I want to do." They were doing all the stuff Blues Incorporated and The Cyril Davis All-Stars were doing, plus numbers The Blue Flames had been doing, but it was by what was, to all intents and purposes, a rock band of young people playing rhythm and blues. They were our age; they were in-yer-face; they were behaving like rock stars – and, unlike Blues Incorporated, it boiled down to electric guitars. It was clear that the Stones were going to Make It as pop stars on those terms, and The Downliners Sect's 40 per cent R&B went up to 100 per cent R&B.'

Actually, it wasn't quite 100 per cent because British R&B was, deduced Craine, 'a very strange animal' – and who could argue when listening to the Sect? Beyond merely sucking Chuck Berry into the vortex of blues as the Stones had, a typical Downliners set might veer fitfully from Berry's 'Too Much Monkey Business' to a skiffle stand-by like 'Wreck Of The Old '97' – and on to exploring Screaming Lord Sutch terrain with, say, the repulsively amusing 'I Want My Baby Back'. In R&B haunts, they trod on thinner ice than the Stones did with Johnny

Cash, via the C&W novelty 'May The Bird Of Paradise Fly Up Your Nose', whose very title may indicate what it was like.

Don Craine had now broadened his instrumental skills with exertions on tambourine and maracas in a line-up that would be completed with the recruitment of mouth organist Ray Sone. Well, the Stones had two in Mick Jagger and, to a far greater degree then, Brian Jones, who was suddenly as recognised a master of blues harmonica as Cyril Davies.

During one Edith Grove afternoon, he had by accident bent a note just like Little Walter did for Muddy Waters. Agreeing maybe with the Confucian adage 'Honour thine error as a hidden intention', he repeated what was technically an error for its tonal impurity, and was able to greet an enthralled Keith, returned from the tobacconist's, with a blues-wailing improvisation from the top of the stairs.

A fractional widening of vibrato during a sustained note on harmonica could be as loaded as any of Jagger's vocal inflections in a given slow blues, as Jones slipped in the space of a few bars from suppressed lust through lazy insinuation to intimate anguish as comfortably as he could with his bottleneck's undulating shiver.

Brian was as much the public face of the group as Mick in those days, and was treated as more than that now the Stones were hot property, and the record industry's search for, if not *the* New Beatles, then *a* New Beatles was shifting from Liverpool and the north back to the more convenient capital. The Stones were being wooed by Georgio Gomelsky, for whom it was a foregone conclusion that they would melt into his managerial caress. After all, since taking them on at the Craw Daddy, he had been doing whatever willingness and energy would do to advance their cause.

First, Georgio had pulled strings so that IBC, a central London studio recommended by Ian Stewart, waived charging the group by the hour in exchange for first refusal on the rights to the five items completed. Brian was to be particularly proud of this session, which caught the Stones when he was very much in charge. It benefited, too, from the precocious console skills of 20-year-old Glyn Johns, no regimented clock-watcher anyway. He'd also heard and liked the Stones at the Craw Daddy, and said as much to IBC proprietor Eric Robinson, a sort of British Mantovani, whose string-laden, middle-aged muzak oozed regularly from the Light Programme.

If just turned 30 himself, Gomelsky didn't expect one such as Robinson to go ape over the Stones, but he had high hopes of Albert Hand, editor of *Teenbeat Monthly*, who was invited to one of the newly instigated lunchtime sessions so he could see for himself that something incredible was taking place at the Station Hotel.

Hand spoke to Jones and Jagger afterwards, but 'the sum total of their conversation was that they were pulling in big crowds at the pub, that they couldn't get a recording contract, and what a big old wicked world it was. They were strange characters, and they had a sort of built-in resentment of the general attitude of showbusiness.'[4]

As a power on the National Jazz Federation, Gomelsky had cultivated all manner of further vital connections, most recently with Brian Epstein, The Beatles' manager, now uprooted from Liverpool to London. This manifested itself most tangibly when Georgio engineered a trip to the Craw Daddy by The Beatles after they'd plugged their new single, 'From Me To You', on the *Thank Your Lucky Stars* pop show at ITV's Teddington studios on 21 April 1963. It would be a fillip for the Stones if they impressed an act who were already bigger than Adam Faith. Yet, though they attracted a small cluster of tongue-tied fans, John Lennon, Paul McCartney, George Harrison and Ringo Starr were not yet so well known around London that they couldn't be steered safely by Gomelsky through the crowded Craw Daddy to the side of the stage.

As Georgio had foreseen, their more revered peers took a shine to the Stones. John Lennon's dockside mouth organ on The Beatles' first three smashes had had hardly a trace of Little Walter *et al*, but he loved all roots and branches of blues, and was keen to pick up tips from Brian on how to improve his 'blowing and sucking'. The cordiality between the two outfits after the customers left the Craw Daddy concluded with the Stones receiving complimentary tickets and 'Access all areas' passes for *Swinging '63*, an all-styles-served-here pop extravaganza headlined by The Beatles, at London's Royal Albert Hall.

'Brian wanted to be a pop star the minute he saw The Beatles,' sneered Keith Richards[5] – and, in the Kensington twilight afterwards, Jones tasted a morsel of ersatz Beatlemania when, because of his moptop, some girls mistook him for George Harrison and asked for his autograph.

Noting Brian's peculiar exaltation at this incident, Georgio pressed home the point that he was at least acquainted with the manoeuvres necessary to give the Stones extra pushes up the ladder, maybe all the way up if the time came. The king of the Craw Daddy imagined, too, that he had also amassed the experience to sidestep most quagmires of the music business, but in coaxing not The Beatles but the less illustrious Albert Hand and other journalists to the club, Gomelsky set in motion a chain of events whereby The Rolling Stones would slip through his fingers.

With the benefit of hindsight, Hand would be one of many claiming with quiet pride to have been the first to mention the Stones to Andrew Loog Oldham, soon to be one of about half a dozen pop svengalis in Britain who truly counted for anything.

Slightly built Andrew was then only just 19 – younger than any of the Stones – but, following the rigours of expensive boarding schools, had been hovering round the industry in mostly menial capacities as a preparation for a grander, but yet unknown purpose. Though he toyed fleetingly with trying to be a pop singer himself, he elected instead to shadow comprehensively the methodology of both those from the old school of showbusiness management and those not inclined to adhere to its lodged conventions.

When briefly a cog in Brian Epstein's publicity machine, Oldham had understood more deeply than many a more battle-hardened talent scout that Epstein's manipulation of The Beatles and his other chart-busting acts was the tip of an iceberg that would make more fortunes than had ever been known in the history of recorded sound.

Oldham felt ready, therefore, to go for the jugular as soon as he'd found a Beatles-sized vehicle with which to do so. He intended also to produce its records and be more than the usual *éminence grise* behind merchandising ballyhoo. He didn't know much about R&B, but he did know what he'd like to exploit – and the Stones seemed as likely to be the next Titans of Teen as any other in this new breed of guitar groups.

He was convinced that he'd struck lucky – and been a nose ahead of an oncoming rush – when, a week after The Beatles had been spared the giggling indignity of queueing for admission to the Craw Daddy, Oldham merged into the middle distance between the nodding 'appreciation' at the back and the massed females positioned stage front to better gawk at Brian ('an incredible blond, hulking hunk'[6]), Mick and, in more qualified fashion, the other three.

There followed a week of private anxiety. As Andrew had neither the cash to launch the Stones nationally nor the clout to enchant record-company representatives or James Grant, producer of *Saturday Club*, to listen to him, Oldham was nevertheless accompanied by someone with both these assets to another Craw Daddy sweat-bath the following Sunday, 28 April.

Eric Easton wasn't an obvious person to supplicate as a possible co-manager. Balding, and nearing his 40s, this former end-of-the-pier organist ran a cautious West End booking agency. His clients veered towards the middle-of-the-road, including as they did Bert Weedon and sing-along pub pianist Mrs Mills – for whom Easton had secured respective residencies on ITV's *Five O'Clock Club* children's series and BBC television's weekly *Billy Cotton Band Show*. On the plus side, however, on his books too was Brian Matthew, presenter of not only *Saturday Club* but *Thank Your Lucky Stars*, for which, pullovered and *sans* tie, he was as casually dressed as he could be without being called to task by the staider ITV programme planners, or Eric Easton, who hadn't let personal dislike of the more transient pop stars and their teenage devotees prevent him from turning a hard-nosed penny when the opportunity knocked.

Eric was perfectly aware, thank you, that the hunt was up for beat groups with sheepdog fringes who, if required, could crank out 'Money', 'Poison Ivy' and the rest of the Merseybeat standards plus a good half of the Chuck Berry songbook. One of these could be recorded in a few takes and released as a single. Why shouldn't another variation on the format of two guitars, bass and drums catch on like others of its kind?

At the Craw Daddy, therefore, Easton, while he stuck out like a sore thumb in his unfashionable suit and flat northern vowels, didn't behave as either an unsmiling pedant or as if visiting another planet. Neither did he eliminate the Stones from the running as a New Beatles – though he wasn't sure what someone like Jimmy Grant, Norrie

Paramor at EMI or Dick Rowe at Decca would feel about that grotesque-looking lead singer and his half-caste nasalings.

Mind you, old Dick had pulled some bold strokes lately. For a while, he'd even left Decca to freelance for the independent Top Rank, for whom he provided a flagship act in John Leyton. When the label folded, he was restored as head of Artists and Repertoire (A&R) at Decca, where he ministered to further hit-parade entries. Why, only in February, his 'Diamonds' for ex-Shadows Jet Harris and Tony Meehan had been at Number One.

However, for all his Top 10 penetrations stretching back to the mid-1950s, Rowe was to earn a historical footnote as The Man Who Turned Down The Beatles after their exploratory session at Decca's West Hampstead complex on New Year's Day 1962. His grounds for doing so were that 'four-piece groups with guitars are finished'. In fairness, executives with other companies were just as blinkered, but – provoked by his failed Scouse supplicants' infuriating success with EMI – a chastised but cynical Rowe had been saturating Decca with artists from the same region. In January alone, he'd made off from Liverpool with The Big Three, Beryl Marsden, singing Cavern disc jockey Billy Butler and, because their drummer had once been a Beatle, Lee Curtis And The All-Stars.

Easton could foresee the Merseybeat ferry grounding on a mud bank before the year was out, and Decca therefore might be persuaded that the Stones were big fish to hook. He had realised already that major structural adjustments might be necessary, but, whatever doubts Eric had about Mick Jagger, his young sidekick was more uncertain about the Stones' pianist. Oldham didn't question the playing, but, to put it bluntly, Stewart's face didn't fit. To drummer Jim McCarty, two months away from joining The Yardbirds, 'Ian always reminded me of "Hoss Cartwright" in *Bonanza*.' A comparison to the obese and dim-witted character in the 1960s cowboy series is unkind, but another consideration was Oldham's: 'I didn't know a really successful group with six people in it. Peter Jay and the Jaywalkers? Cliff Bennett and the Rebel Rousers? The public can't count up to six.'[6]

It was thought prudent to thrust such misgivings aside during that second visit to the Craw Daddy. The usually dapper Oldham had also heeded the advice of Percy Dickins, co-founder of the *NME*, to dress down a bit if he was to effuse credibility as would-be manager of The Rolling Stones.

He and Eric spoke at first to Charlie Watts, who continued dismantling his kit after calling over the Stone they'd heard addressed as 'Brian' to see what these two blokes wanted. 'Brian was the one we had to negotiate with,'[7] said Oldham, noting that Jones at least had the good manners to be civil to him and Easton when the latter bought a round of drinks and suggested a formal meeting at the agency office. Shall we say two o'clock on Tuesday?

He arrived with Mick Jagger in tow, and did most of the talking on his own and the group's behalf, hearing fine words when Andrew put them on a par with The Beatles. For Brian, the principal outcome was that he could wash his hands of the begging letters, cold telephone calls and ensuring that musicians and equipment were in the same place at the same time. The offstage machinations that were as crucial as his playing were no longer his responsibility. Something may have warned him that loss of responsibility equalled loss of power, that he was conceding a defeat in his acceptance of a subordinate administrative role in the new regime, but the overall feeling was one of relief. It was a moment, seemingly of open-handed affability, that stuck in Andrew Loog Oldham's memory: 'Brian sat across from Eric Easton and began the long goodbye.'[6]

Brian's *de facto* leadership of the Stones might have been tacitly over that day, but it would appear as if nothing was amiss at the beginning of May, when it was he who signed the official agreement, permitting Oldham and Easton's freshly founded Impact Sound management company to take official charge of his Rolling Stones' professional lives for the next three years.

The next hurdle was Georgio Gomelsky, who had been harmlessly across the Channel, attending to a family bereavement, when Oldham and Easton had pounced. Saddened by what he saw as the group reneging on 'a verbal understanding, I felt tremendously let down'. Neither could he be blamed for hurling a metaphorical stone at the departing back of the one he had no serious doubt had been the deception's central character: 'I never like to work with monsters, no matter how talented. Jones should have had treatment. His responses were never those of a normal person.'[7]

Following any signpost that pointed in the direction of fame and wealth, Brian was quite prepared to sacrifice Mick and Ian, too, if needs must. 'Easton said to Brian, "I don't think Jagger is any good",' snarled Stewart, 'and so Brian said, "OK, we'll just get rid of him." I felt sure Brian would have done it. I said to him, "Don't be so bloody daft."'[7]

Nothing had been resolved with regard to who was and who wasn't a Rolling Stone when George Harrison was judging a 'Battle Of The Bands'-type tournament at his native Liverpool's Philharmonic Hall on 10 May. On the panel, too, were Bill Harry, editor of *Mersey Beat*, and soul-tortured Dick Rowe. Whispering to Harrison sitting next to him, Rowe reckoned that none of the contestants were better or worse than any other Beatles-style outfit to be found anywhere in the country.

Civilly, George agreed. Because Dick had been honest in not over-justifying his error in turning his nose up at the Beatles' audition tape, George decided to help him out. There was, he said, this southern group he'd seen. Musically, they were 'almost as good as The Roadrunners'[8] (which, prior to tainting their act with too much Scouse humour, they might have been). This other lot, enthused Harrison, were far wilder visually, and having the same effect on their audience in a provincial club as The Beatles had on theirs at the celebrated Cavern. 'Dick got up immediately,' observed Bill Harry, 'and caught the next train back to sign The Rolling Stones.'

Perhaps Eric Easton had imagined it, but there'd been a sufficiently strident note of urgency in Dick Rowe's streets-of-Islington whine to propel him and young Andrew to Decca's riverside offices, where the normally hoity-toity receptionist conducted them straight away into the presence of the managing director. He and Dick Rowe knew the type they were dealing with in Eric Easton, but neither knew what to make of young Oldham, sprawled disrespectfully in a button-leather armchair, with his fast mouth and his sweeping aside of such obstacles as demo tapes and auditions. They could keep their West Hampstead studios, he told them. The Stones would be taping their first record and those that came after elsewhere. Furthermore, they wouldn't need a Decca staff producer, either. He'd take care of all that.

In a half-nelson because the Stones' pressure-cooker reputation was steaming too fast from the Craw Daddy, Decca had no choice but to fix a ghastly corporate smile as this dreadful teenage upstart called the shots and third-degreed the boss. Decca didn't want the next Beatles to go with Pye, Philips or, heaven forbid, an EMI subsidiary, did it? By the weekend, a three-year Decca recording deal guaranteed the Stones and their handlers a royalty of six per cent between them – a lot more than EMI had granted their precious Beatles.

As it had been with the Impact Sound document, Brian's was the only Stone signature on the contract. He was also the only member of the group there when it was decided how the assorted and incoming monies would be divided. The others were too overwhelmed by the speed of events to investigate – or even find out – why Jones, still clinging onto a yet unruffled dignity as bandleader, had winkled out of Easton an extra few pounds a week for himself.

Andrew Oldham's only interest in Brian's little display of avarice was storing the information away for use against him if the situation arose. There was a more immediate problem – and Jones could help solve it: 'After everything was signed, they remembered the session Gomelsky had set up. The deal gave IBC a specific time period in which to do something with these tapes. So we rehearsed Brian to go to them and say he felt the band was going nowhere, and that he had this big opportunity to join some other outfit. Could IBC let him go if he paid back the £106 in studio costs – and they fell for it, thank God.'[7]

If Eric Easton anticipated little more than a detached professional relationship with his new clients, the inherent comedy of Brian's IBC mission sealed further an affinity based as much on friendship as profit between the younger partner and the majority of the Stones.

Brian, however, had been at loggerheads with Andrew in less than a week after the ratification of the Impact Sound contract. When the group assembled at the Decca block for publicity photographs along the Albert Embankment, Brian brought along the now-seldom-seen Pat and Mark. Though they stood out of lens range, the mere existence of a 'common-law wife' and toddler percolated Oldham's rage that Jones had transgressed to the *nth* degree the rule that still applies to all male pop idols, whether post-bellum Johnnie Ray or Will Young at the start of the third millennium – which was to play down abiding romantic attachments that would tarnish their appeal to girls. Marty Wilde had inflicted untold damage to his career by a very public wedding to one of The Vernon Girls and a consequent revelling in his married state. For that reason, John Lennon – to Brian Epstein's sly satisfaction – not only stayed well within the bounds of acceptable ickiness with regard to his own missus, but also emitted subliminal signals that he was still discreetly 'available'.

Andrew Oldham, therefore, watched sourly as Brian compounded the felony after the photo shoot when, said Pat, 'we all went across to Battersea Park funfair, and Brian was carrying Mark on his shoulder. We put him into the crèche, and afterwards went to buy him some trousers. The next day, Brian was called into Andrew's office and told that under no circumstances was he ever to be seen in public with Mark again. Brian went absolutely ballistic.'

Jones kept his fists, if not his words, in check. Thankful for smaller mercies, Oldham was glad, too, that Brian wasn't actually living with this woman any more – though there'd been a flickering indication that the danger hadn't passed when, recounted Pat, 'I went into hospital – St George's in Ladbroke Grove – in April 1963 with peritonitis before going back to Cheltenham for two weeks to convalesce. Then I thought, "Blow it! I'm going back to Brian." That Saturday, I went to the Ealing club. Brian was there, and it was, ostensibly, just like I'd never been gone, but our relationship was based on friendship more than anything else – probably because Brian had nobody else. I was the one person who'd been close to him before the Stones started to happen. We were from the same town. Yet, though I loved Brian, I was no longer in love with him – and we became very good friends.'

This emotional sea change coupled with Pat viewing Cheltenham through a rosier haze, following that spring fortnight of clean sheets and Mum's home cooking. Just as the Stones' first single reached the pressing plant, she and Mark left London for a much longer while to the sound of Andrew Loog Oldham emptying his lungs with a *whoosh*.

7 Devil In Disguise

'Brian had more edge to him than any of the others then. He was the nasty one. He could be really evil on stage.'

– Alexis Korner [1]

It was a cover of 'Come On', a Chuck Berry B-side a few weeks old, but gingered up mainly with Brian's *wah-wah-wah* harmonica ostinato that, if essentially monotonal, had to negotiate a corny but tricky key change for the last verse. To the Craw Daddy crowd, it was hardly a show stopper, and a *Record Mirror* feature-cum-review confirmed that 'it's not the fanatical R&B sound that audiences wait hours to hear'.[2] However, spins on the Light Programme and more muffled airings on Radio Luxembourg allied with the buzz from London to begin a yo-yo progression to the edge of the Top 20, where it lingered until autumn, so fulfilling *Record Mirror*'s prophecy that it 'should make the charts in a small way'.[2]

Now flinging beat groups at the public almost indiscriminately, Decca often neglected the promotional needs of all but those that already had some sort of future. Chief among these during 1963's unsettled summer was Brian Poole And The Tremeloes, whose fifth single, 'Twist And Shout', was at Number Four. They were respected by company executives as a yardstick of professionalism: *Saturday Club* regulars; dependable in the studio as both session players and in their own right; neatly coiffeured; garbed in not-too-way-out stage suits and given to stage patter that didn't include swearing or overt attempts to pull front-row girls – everything a decent pop group ought to be.

It made naive sense to smooth The Rolling Stones into a similar shape. They'd done well for first-timers, but who could yet presume, said Decca, that they were anything other than a classic local group who'd caught the lightning once and would probably be back on the factory bench by this time next year? So it was that Brian, Mick, Keith, Bill and Charlie were each squeezed into a costume of shiny waistcoat, white shirt, dark tie, black trousers and Cuban-heeled boots for a photo shoot with Brian Poole and his lads to indicate, shrugged Poole 'that they were joining the Decca "family", I suppose'.

Ian Stewart could wear what he liked, because under no circumstances was he to be seen either in photographs of the group or on the boards with them anymore. It was a cruel necessity, but he'd remain part of the team, so Brian assured him – as if Brian was still in a position to do so. Ian could be the road manager.

His pride smarted, but it would be more humiliating to go back to the day job he'd given up to 'turn professional'. So Stewart swallowed the insult, and looked on as The Tremeloes and the apparently lower-ranking Stones arranged themselves standing in a half-circle behind the two Brians in pride of place on stools. Poole in his jacket appeared to be imparting gesticulating advice to the waistcoated Jones, jovial voice of experience to an earnest young shaver, who'd portrayed himself as a former 'architect' in his earliest remarks to the national music press.[2]

Still toeing an amenable line, the Jones group traced the Brian Poole scent to *Saturday Club* and, on 7 July 1963, also made a televisual debut, miming 'Come On' on *Thank Your Lucky Stars*. This warranted a promotion to matching check coats with velvet collars, but sartorial uniformity was abandoned forever as these acquired frayed cuffs and indelible stains born of sweat and spillage during not so much a Rolling Stones tour as a continual and sporadic string of one-nighters, commencing in Middlesbrough's Alcove Club on 13 June, and concentrated mainly on eastern England.

Owing to the meritocratic nature of a profession based on chart performances, there were support spots to such as The Hollies, on the wings of their second hit, but the Stones' solitary Top 30 strike allowed them to lord it over a diversity of other acts, though a handful gave cause for nervous backwards glances. Preceding the Stones at Morecambe's Floral Hall – one of only two west coast engagements –

The Merseybeats and Dave Berry both happened to enter the lower reaches of the Top 50 for the first time in the same September week, Dave with 'Memphis Tennessee', a Chuck Berry number of fresher vintage than 'Come On'.

Somewhere else, Wayne Fontana And The Mindbenders also leaned heavily on rhythm and blues and earned Brian's approbation – qualified, because he preferred the US blueprints – but other couplings weren't so concordant when pop music was still seen as an offshoot of light entertainment. 'There weren't any subdivisions then,' said Dave Berry. 'There would have been nothing unusual for the Stones to have been on the same bill as a crooner, an instrumental group or a singing postman. No one thought any of the new groups would last, as there was no precedent. It was the first real wave of true British pop, and no one could guess what was in store.'

John Keen caught a glimmer when peep-parping in one of the trad outfits booked for the third National Jazz Festival, held in a Richmond sports ground one Sunday in August, and leavened with more than a pinch of R&B. 'We were doing an afternoon spot,' he recalled, 'and there weren't many there, but then I noticed a huge queue waiting for the next act, all young people. Well, the next act on was The Rolling Stones.

'I spoke to Brian after their set, and he told me things were really taking off for the band, and he said they had a hit at Number 17 [*sic*] in the charts. Then he introduced me to the rest of the band, and what struck me was that they all wore great clothes – very smart Italian suits, shirts and ties, winkle-picker shoes… I knew then that Brian had taken a different path since Cheltenham, because jazzers were always scruffy.'[3]

Whatever favourable impression they made on John Keen, the Stones' first venture outside the underground security of the Home Counties' R&B circuit was often thankless. Partly, it was self-inflicted. They'd come to loathe 'Come On' and refused to play it even if specifically requested by onlookers, who expected to hear a given chart contender's hits for five bob (25p/40c) and said so in between songs. The luxury of self-indulgence invited catcalls and outbreaks of barracking. As well as their verbal retaliations to same, the Stones' cissy long hair (ie barely touching their collars – especially Brian's and Mick's) was another red rag for patrons of this East Anglian Corn Exchange or that seaside ballroom for whom even quiffed Elvis was not yet a symbol of masculinity.

Jones stoked up the most aggression with a studied radiation of anti-everything menace laced with effeminacy, sensed by factions in the crowd as they would the 'evil' from the syndicated peroxide-framed eyes of the late child murderer Myra Hindley three years later. Back in the safety of the Craw Daddy, Alexis Korner had seen for himself how 'Brian went out to needle people, to really arouse them, so that they really responded. You'd see him dancing forward with a tambourine and snapping it in your face and sticking his tongue out at you in a nasty way, not in a schoolboyish way – and then he'd move back before you actually took a punch at him.'[1]

Jubilantly, Jones, then and later, would point out the pockets of violence he'd incited and, grimaced photographer Gered Mankowitz, 'always seemed ready for some sort of confrontation with the police when concerts got out of hand'.[4] More insidiously aggravating were the quietly narcissistic endeavours as he pretended that he couldn't care less about the more-than-passive interest of the girls near the front, tits bouncing, and, further back, lads who, bold with beer and heterosexual bluster, daren't admit finding the Stones' nancy-boy general factotum guiltily transfixing as, by slightly overdoing the subliminal obnoxiousness, he wallowed in a repellent bewitchment. Afterwards, entranced converts vanished into the night, lost in wonder. Years of incomprehension, lamentation, deprivation, uproar, interminable 'atmospheres' and altercation would follow.

Confident that he was the Stones' principal spokesman as well as their chief show-off, a gradually more irritating trait to the other Stones was Brian butting into conversations in order to imprint his importance to the group on outsiders. As if he alone controlled its destiny, he'd pontificate publicly and often ignorantly about matters yet to be discussed with the others, and say 'we' instead of 'I'.

'We don't want to play at the Star-Club,' he confided airily to Richard Green of the *NME*. 'This is because British groups are only booked there to fill in. The club features American names, and British outfits that have appeared there have not starred.'[5] Admittedly, The Beatles had been the main attraction on the very opening night in 1962 of the legendary Hamburg nightspot, which then sought out further Britons to do the same, even hosting a week-long 'Liverpool Festival' featuring nothing but entertainers from northwest England's grimy pivot of industrial enterprise.

It was Jones whose borderline sarcasm was to bring the drip-drip of muttered fulminations between the Stones and Liverpool's Swinging Blue Jeans close to fisticuffs before an ebbing away that left the combatants glowering at each other from opposite ends of a BBC canteen. This contradicted the sweetness-and-light Brian had brought into play when the Stones' van ran out of petrol at gone midnight in a Welsh country lane narrow enough to oblige the sounding of the horn at every bend. It was also too lonely a road to expect to find a telephone booth. Brian took up the story in the *NME*: 'So there we were, wandering about, trying to think of a way of getting some juice, when along came a policeman on a bike. After searching the van for mail bags, he ended up by helping us shove it to a farm. I reckon they should call it the strong arm, not the long arm of the law.'[6]

Most amusing, I'm sure – though how did Louise Jones feel when Brian, whose infant digits she had guided through so many piano exercises, wrote 'self-taught' under 'musical education' when the Stones filled the *NME*'s 'Lifelines' tabulation – height, weight, favourite colour, hobbies *et al* – even if Bach was among his 'favourite composers' (the others were Muddy Waters and Lennon-McCartney)? Moreover, she and Lewis alone couldn't pretend his hobby of 'women'[7] was penned in jest. They knew their son well enough to not quite shut from their minds imagined carnal shenanigans with stage-door Jezebels that took place in the romantic seclusion of, say, a backstage broom cupboard on the Stones' first proper round-Britain tour – 30-odd dates beginning on 29 September, low on the bill to the all-American Everly Brothers, Bo Diddley and, contracted after the first posters had been printed, Little Richard.

Wisely, shadowy thighs and lewd sniggering did not leap out of the pages of Brian's letters to his fretting parents and the more frequent postcards to his latest flame, Linda Lawrence, whom he'd met during the Stones' run of several summer Tuesdays in Windsor's Ricky Tick club. The daughter of a local builder, she was worth a second glance, for she had a figure that suggested that a career of catwalks and cloth was on the cards as well as an alluring combination of a shy, pixie-like smile that showed off her fine teeth, and a steady gaze from the depths of a fringe of the blackest hair. On closer acquaintance, Brian had been struck further by a tranquillity in Linda, a 'bird' so different from more brazen species that he chased until they caught him. He had wondered if sex would spoil things between them, but suppressed the thought immediately.

To a besotted Linda's relief, he'd closed the door on an old love a week into the tour. 'When the Stones came to Cheltenham, I thought, OK, I'll go,' said Pat Andrews. 'I didn't have any money, but I'd made friends with some firemen, who were in attendance at the show. They said they'd get me in. So I sat four or five rows from the front, waiting for Little Richard and Bo Diddley to come on. I wasn't going to scream at the Stones, as I'd seen them a hundred times before.

'During the interval, Ian Stewart found me and said that Brian wanted me to come backstage. Once again, it was almost like Brian and I had seen each other only yesterday, and he said, "Do us a favour. Go across the road and get me some fags." All the other Stones fumbled in their pockets for change so I could buy them cigarettes, too.

'Brian wasn't leaving until the next afternoon, and arranged to meet me in town. It hadn't reached the stage where he was being pestered – or even recognised – in daylight, so we walked around, had something to eat, and were together until about three o'clock before he had to leave for the next gig. That was the last I ever saw of him.'

It was goodbye to Richard Hattrell, too. 'After the Cheltenham show, I tracked Brian down to the Waikiki, a club patronised by the town's trendiest people. He was completely on his own in the corner. I gathered there'd been some quarrel earlier with one of the others, probably Keith, and Brian was very unhappy, very fed up, but he invited me down to a private after-hours session in the hotel where he was staying. I never saw him again after that.'

A date towards the end of the tour – at Rochester's Odeon cinema – was close enough for Linda Lawrence to attend. So did a certain Mick

Jones and his then-girlfriend, Linda Hollis. Arriving early, they crossed the road to a pub. Leaving her Babycham, Miss Hollis visited the toilet through the saloon bar. On completing her ablutions, she told Mick she'd just seen 'a bunch of beatniks'.

Mick's account of the rest of the evening is worth quoting at length: 'My response was to tell her not to be silly. There weren't any beatniks in Rochester. Then it dawned. It was a fair bet that it was the Stones. Only recently, I'd read that the Stones respected Bo Diddley, and wouldn't be playing his material – although they usually did – and that they were avid blues fans.

'Anyway, I had no more considered it than I was in the saloon with hardly a "Won't be a minute, love." Upon opening the door, immediately before me were two tables pulled together with what must have been ten people around them. Sure enough, I recognised three of them as members of the Stones. Brian Jones, Bill Wyman and Charlie Watts were with some other guys – and some girls who I especially remember as having long straight hair – something I'd not been used to seeing around Rochester.

'I said in what must have been an aggressive tone, "Are you The Rolling Stones?" and Wyman looked up lazily and said, "You might say that." Then I commenced to raise my objections to their claims to being bluesmen, feeling they weren't worthy of wiping Muddy Waters' shoes. As I was saying this, I heard my words as if they were from another's mouth, and I wondered what on earth had possessed me to put myself in this position. I mean, I was effectively slagging them off – and there were six or seven blokes looking at me. When I'd ended my tirade, I blurted out pathetically, "Hope you don't think I'm having a go."

'Brian said to me, smiling, "No, of course not" – and I have forever been indebted to him for that kindness to an undeserving stranger. He then got chatting to me quite amiably, and even asked if I was going to the show. When I replied that I was, he asked, "Why don't you shout something out to us – like 'Get yer 'air cut!'?" "What, and get some prearranged remark back?" Jones laughed, and said, "Yes, that's the idea." I thought then that it was time to beat a retreat. I've since heard that that suggested shout was used in a film of those times by either someone genuine or a plant. On the film, Brian shouts back, "What – and look like you?"'

Though it had flowed to Screaming Lord Sutch's shoulders since 1959, the group's hair was already causing comment. 'I think it's longer than mine,' quipped Julie Grant,[8] an Eric Easton client since a childhood of talent-contest victories. There'd been viewers' complaints as far back as June after the Stones – even a Stones, as smart as they could be – had flashed into living rooms on *Thank Your Lucky Stars*. 'We don't grow our hair like this for a gimmick,' Brian had protested in the *NME* the following month. 'But we see no reason why we should cut it off to conform.'[9]

Today's ponytailed navvy would find it incredible that 'Well, he had long hair, hadn't he?' had been the plea of a man at Aldershot Magistrates Court accused of beating up a complete stranger in early 1964 as the issue gathered speed. Even when it became acceptable for studs to grow it longer than a crew cut, you could still invite persecution from those whose brusque trims were governed by work conditions. 'Peter's pride was his shoulder-length hair,' chortled a write-up in the *Daily Express*, in early 1964, about the scalping of a teenager by British soldiers garrisoned in Cyprus.[10]

Peter would have sympathised with a Farnborough Grammar pupil who would be held fast while his nape-length locks were hacked off by some 'manly' types in safe assurance of leniency from an arsehole of a deputy head called 'Trunky' Cotgreave – for whom hair had become as touchy a subject as it was for those he victimised. Of the same kidney was Donald Thompson, head teacher of Coventry's Woodlands Comprehensive, who, in May 1964, was to suspend 11 boys for sporting 'long and scruffy Rolling Stones styles', permitting their return if they trimmed down to at least Beatle length.[11]

As well as listing 'having a shower' as his only entry in 'Miscellaneous likes' in 'Lifelines',[7] Brian Jones also had his hair cut more regularly than his denigrators imagined. Rather than to a barber who might be prompted by an inner devil to make a snip too far, the duty fell to girlfriends made aware that any mistake would be comparable to a medical emergency. As the operation neared completion, Brian's eyes would widen and he'd be speechless in an unremitting contemplation of his own beauty. On the recent jaunt, Brian would be the Stone sighted most often preening himself in the dressing-room mirror (if there was one). On one occasion, he elected to wash his hair in a hand-basin ten minutes before showtime, causing a half-hour delay. Well, there was no point, was there, in mounting the boards unless you looked like a million dollars? The fans expected it.

'Success went to Brian's head immediately,' glowered Keith Richards, 'and the more successful we became, the more it interfered with his compatibility within the band.'[12] Onstage instances had been noted of Brian bucking and gyrating as if he had a wasp in his pants, as if infused with an attention-grabbing desire to outdo Mick. This was easy to do then, as Jagger – whose movements were often limited anyway by small stages and an undetachable skull-like chrome microphone on a heavy stand – revealed only half-hidden clues of the showman he was to become.

Brian's antics beneath the proscenium came into sharper focus on the Everly Brothers tour, notably when George Harrison turned up disguised in a hat and beard on the night that considered ovations had unfurled into screams. Thus a pattern was set, though the Stones remained on a billing equal to that of Julie Grant, whom Eric Easton visualised as a rival to fading schoolgirl pop star Helen Shapiro. The last of Julie's three small chart entries had stopped just short of the Top 30, but there'd been high hopes of her just-issued 'Hello Love'.

By the final night, 'Hello Love' had died its death, while The Everly Brothers were conducting themselves with observed good humour, eclipsed as they been most of the time by the home-grown group whose fans had hurled paper cups and bawled 'We want the Stones!' even as the pompadoured duo pitched into 'Bye Bye Love', *risqué* 'Wake Up Little Susie', 1961's chart-topping 'Temptation' and further smashes as old as the hills.

They hadn't a prayer from the start. Their last three releases had been relative flops, while the Stones had been buoyed mid-tour by a picked-to-click second single, 'I Wanna Be Your Man', a Lennon-McCartney opus, with Brian to the fore with a bottleneck solo, that would peak just outside the Top 10 as Diddley's 'Pretty Thing' would at Number 34, a UK chart debut that also elevated him to more than a cult celebrity in

Britain.[13] Brian would treasure the memory of 'actually playing harmonica with Bo Diddley. You don't forget the day a long-standing dream comes true'[14] – though Bill Wyman would recollect Jones's non-arrival at the *Saturday Club* session where this was supposed to have taken place.

If less revered by the Stones than Diddley, the energetic Little Richard, 'The Georgia Peach', had had considerably more commercial success. Following a breakthrough with 'Tutti Frutti' in 1955, he had remained a chart fixture for the next three years with such rock 'n' roll set works as 'Rip It Up,' 'Long Tall Sally' and 1958's 'Good Golly Miss Molly' – all dominated by Richard's vamping piano and declamatory vocal. However, he had gained only one minor hit since taking holy orders in 1959, but, like a batty favourite uncle, neither sinister nor sexy, he was received with an affection that was not extended to The Everly Brothers.

The screams murmured in Brian's ears as if from a seashore conch as he eased himself between the sheets in his bed and breakfast and the others spent as comfortable a night as was feasible in their more spartan digs. Outside, milk floats braved an icy dawn, and a snowdrift blocked the twisty lane in Wales where the Stones had come to a sudden halt a few weeks earlier. Still short of ready cash and with palates becoming coarsened by chips-with-everything meals in wayside snack bars, they ingratiated themselves with others in the tour cast. 'I was impressed with how polite they were,' beamed Julie Grant. 'They were always very nice to me and my Mum, who was my chaperone with me being only seventeen. They didn't have much money, and on one occasion, my Mum gave them and Andrew Oldham some money for fish-and-chips.'[15]

Ignorant of the Stones' living and travelling conditions on the road, it was encouraging for newer groups scrimmaging round the unsalubrious R&B clubs that were now littering every major town, that Jones, Jagger *et al* had breathed the air around Bo Diddley, notched up another hit *and* been on *Thank Your Lucky Stars* again. What's more, they'd done so this time without compromising a hirsute, motley image, even if, on the same TV channel, they hadn't been above soundtracking a Rice Krispies commercial that endured from autumn 1963 to the following spring,[16] and raised their thumbs in photographed endorsement of Vox amplifiers.[17] Whether motivated to help the needy or not, they also did their bit in a charity match against Julie Grant's Teenstar Bowling League 'with Patsy Ann Noble, The Fourmost, Stu James of The Mojos, Jess Conrad and many more,' said Julie. 'The Stones also donated sacks of toys to children's hospitals.'[15]

If Nice Lads When You Get To Know Them – the angle adopted by every pop star from Johnnie Ray to Oasis – the Stones had shown that you no longer had to dress the same and make yuck-for-a-buck singles to Hit The Big Time. As for staying up there, well, you'd have to cross that bridge when you came to it.

Just look at Dave Berry and his backing Cruisers, shackled to local orbits in the northeast for three years before The Break came, when they were scrutinised by Mickie Most at a Doncaster Baths booking with Freddie And The Dreamers. This freelance producer put them before Decca, whose A&R lieutenant, Mike Smith, found Most's plans for them unworkable. Therefore, it was Smith himself who issued orders from the glass-fronted booth of tape spools and switches when the Cruisers and Berry assembled to make their maiden single in the summer of 1963.

There were no grumbles about the Top 20 placing of 'Memphis Tennessee' – albeit far below the Chuck Berry original. However, when the second 45, a revival of Elvis Presley-via-Arthur Crudup's 'My Baby Left Me', stalled at Number 37, a change of strategy was in order. The Sheffield bluesman therefore found another voice for 'Baby It's You', a morosity from The Beatles' first album, just as 'I Wanna Be Your Man' had been an uptempo item from the second.

Even more lachrymose than this Top 30 restorative were 'The Crying Game' and its twin, 'One Heart Between Two', heartbreak ballads tailor-made for Berry's cartoon spookiness onstage, hinged on a vague and surreal composite of rock 'n' roll rebel prototype James Dean's Brooding Intensity and Gene Vincent's crippled melodrama. Yet, if the most illustrious young adult in his home region, Berry wasn't beyond being asked to leave Chesterfield's Carlton watering hole because he and his retinue 'looked like beatniks'.

Another Mickie Most 'discovery' were The Animals, formed in 1962 from veterans of diverse skiffle, trad, rock 'n' roll and R&B outfits around

Tyneside. They were seized by EMI – as were The Downliners Sect, who had been taken on as house band at Studio 51 in September 1963 – as The Yardbirds had that same month at the Craw Daddy – while the Stones, zigzagging across the country, decommitted themselves more and more from their grass roots.

There is weighty vinyl evidence that the Sect, not the Stones, were Britain's foremost Bo Diddley interpreters. Yet they, too, were starting to sound and look as disconcertingly like a pop group, and would likewise be in transition from Studio 51 heroes to the national dance-hall circuit as the first step towards world conquest. However, at the California Ballroom, Dunstable, 'We were terrible,' admitted Don Craine, 'but, because they'd never heard of R&B, they gave us the benefit of the doubt.'

Back in London, among those who coveted Sect mouth organist Ray Sone's job were stars-in-waiting Rod Stewart, Steve Marriott and Van Morrison, then in a touring Irish show band, with guitarist Herbie Armstrong, who 'remembered him asking if he could blow harmonica with them, but they said it was too late. I think Van had had the idea of forming an R&B group before that, but when he saw The Downliners Sect, he said "that's the sort of group I want to have!"' Morrison himself corroborated this statement with 'the first British R&B group I heard was The Downliners Sect. It was at the Ken Colyer club. They were really doing it then.'[18] By the finale – an extemporisation of Diddley's 'Nursery Rhyme' – the enraptured young man had decided to quit the Irish show-band scene to form his own R&B group, Them.

The Sect's daring repertoire was among factors that gained them the EMI contract – as an 'answer' to Decca's Stones – after the issue of an atmospheric in-concert EP, *Nite In Great Newport Street*, on an independent shoestring label. EMI talent scouts had been struck, too, by how well the group's diverting and frequently hilarious recitals captivated an enthusiastic following during a residency at Eel Pie Island after the one at Studio 51 ended.

A something-for-everybody policy did not always reconcile readily on disc for the Sect. Though almost as much linchpins of the Greater London wing of the British R&B movement as the Stones, the quintet were to be lost amongst those also-rans they had influenced – units who'd chosen names like The Howling Wolves, The T-Bones, The Primitives, The King Bees, The Mannish Boys and, gawd help us, The Little Boy Blues after ditching Beatle-esque winsomeness for blues-wailing taciturnity, so lending credence to Marquee manager Bill Carey's gripe in *Record Mirror* that 'every beat group with money enough to buy a harmonica and hire a four-chord guitarist is calling itself R&B. It's a cast-iron certainty that, in 1964, the great heaving mound of Tin Pan Alley-controlled beat groups will attach itself to the R&B label.'[19]

The usual summit of short careers was a trivial round of local engagements and a smattering of airplay for one, maybe two, singles that demonstrated musical ability at odds with overweening expressive ambition before the perpetrators made a proper go of their day jobs, instead of yearning for any more glittering alternative that might result, however indirectly, from the next feedback-ridden, drum-thudding evening.

That's, more or less, what happened to The Primitives, despite a respectable go at Sonny Boy Williamson's 'Help Me' at a time when most would-be UK bluesmen copying the Sonny Boys, Muddy Waters and Howlin' Wolfs of this world were discovering that the results, especially vocal, weren't anything like.

'Chicago Callin'', the debut 45 by Cyril Davies And His R&B All-Stars, however, almost was – as would be 'Dimples', a John Lee Hooker xerox on 45 by Birmingham's Spencer Davis Group, whose leader was a proficient, even distinctive, singer and guitarist. It was, nonetheless, Spencer Davis's misfortune that his young sidekick, Steve Winwood, if pop-eyed at the microphone, was in another league via an instinctive Brian Jones-like command of any fretboard or keyboard instrument put in front of him – plus a voice of strangled, lived-in passion.

Gravelly ranting was the ace up the sleeve of Joe Cocker, who – under his adolescent stage alias of 'Vance Arnold' – was lauded in the *Sheffield Telegraph* as 'surely a star of the future'[20] after he and his backing Avengers held their own while supporting The Rolling Stones at the Town Hall.

Among those who supported The Downliners Sect, before the going got erratic, was a Muswell Hill ensemble, The Kinks, who were about to be grabbed by Pye. 'Decca turned them down,' snarled co-manager Larry Page, 'because they had the Stones already.'[21]

To Pye's annoyance, The Kinks' first two singles bit the dust. The same was true of Manfred Mann, who likewise traded in worthy and open-ended arrangements of mostly R&B set works – 'Down The Road Apiece', 'Hoochie Coochie Man', 'Mojo Working', 'Route 66', 'Smokestack Lightning' and so forth – at Studio 51, Eel Pie Island and the Marquee. 'Manfred and Mike [Vickers, multi-instrumentalist] were playing in a modern jazz quartet, and decided they weren't going to make a living out of that,' elucidated Paul Jones. 'They had no feeling for rhythm-and-blues, but they knew they didn't want to play rock 'n' roll. So for them it was a compromise between music and money, so when you listen now to the Manfred Mann version of "Smokestack Lightning", you can hear that it's played by musicians who didn't have a terrific amount of feeling for that stuff – but we wanted hits, no two ways about it. We saw those girls screaming at the Stones, and I wanted a piece of that.'[22]

A giant step in that direction was Manfred Mann's acceptance of a commission to come up with a theme for a newish ITV pop series, *Ready Steady Go*, to replace The Surfaris' 'Wipeout'. What emerged was '54321', a catchy if self-mythologising opus that reached the Top 10 before it was even heard on the programme – and before the Stones did – and turned Manfred Mann into as much of a pop group as, say, The Swinging Blue Jeans. Indeed, they weren't above crass publicity photos like one in which Paul Jones, the Mann with the longest hair, is being dragged into a barber's by the others. Nevertheless, Manfred Mann's 'intellectual' image appealed less to wearers of miniskirts than girls who hid their figures inside vast sweaters borrowed from undergraduate boyfriends. After all, when Paul Pond (as was) had sung with Brian Jones, he was fresh from a year at university. Moreover, Mann wore glasses and a beatnik beard – and if that isn't intellectual, then I don't know what is.

Meanwhile, Mike Cooper, now a Manfred Mann lookalike, had formed The Blues Committee which, for all his blues purist ideals, 'ended up doing material that the Stones did'. The Yardbirds, however, 'made a conscious decision not to do the same numbers the Stones did', pronounced drummer Jim McCarty, 'though we drew our repertoire from the same albums by Jimmy Reed, Muddy Waters, Slim Harpo,

Chuck Berry, Howlin' Wolf... The Stones did Harpo's "I'm A King Bee"; we did his "Scratch My Back". We did Wolf's "Smokestack Lightning"; they did "Little Red Rooster" – though we did "Down The Road Apiece", which they recorded eventually, but we never tried "Route 66".'

From the ashes of The Metropolitan Blues Quartet, The Yardbirds had smouldered into form, *circa* mid-1963, with McCarty, singing mouth organist Keith Relf (Jane's brother), Paul Samwell-Smith on bass and guitarists Chris Dreja and Anthony Topham, delivering R&B around the western edge of Greater London. As it had been with Dick Taylor in the Stones, student Topham quit The Yardbirds in the interests of higher education. He was replaced as lead guitarist by the older Eric 'Slowhand' Clapton, late of Casey Jones And The Engineers.

As Them were to be recalled as Van Morrison's old group, so most consumers of today's cultured 'contemporary' pop for the over-40s have taught their children to regard The Yardbirds as less combined figureheads and *éminences grises* of 1960s pop than a springboard for the nurtured prowess and neo-deification of Clapton, who was no more eloquent an instrumentalist than Topham, but possessed stronger stage presence at the Craw Daddy, where his overamplified Fender duelled with Relf's surging harmonica during the 'rave-ups' that convinced both onlookers and contract-waving recording managers that, as The Rolling Stones and Manfred Mann had pushed R&B-derived pop into the hit parade, The Yardbirds were poised to do likewise.

Sniffing round them, too, was Brian Jones, who, according to McCarty, furrowed a half-serious brow about nurturing them for greener pastures as Andrew Loog Oldham had with the Stones, and Bill Wyman, so far as Stones' duties would allow, was contemplating doing with a couple of promising groups he'd checked out recently. Nevertheless, such a liaison between Brian and The Yardbirds progressed no further than an informal chat round Keith and Jane Relf's parents' house in Richmond. 'It was an ego thing for Brian,' reckoned Jim, 'to show that he could cope with both playing with the Stones and managing us, but it fizzled out probably because he realised exactly how much time and money – of which he could spare neither – needed to be invested.'

Brian – and Ian Stewart – were also 'interested' in The Tridents, formerly Nightshift, whose lead guitarist, Jeff Beck, had borrowed from Stewart 1963's *Folk Festival Of The Blues*, an aural souvenir of a Chicago concert the previous summer showcasing Muddy Waters, Howlin' Wolf, Buddy Guy and Sonny Boy Williamson II. However, Beck was prone to 'going off on a tangent, and everyone would laugh and say, "Play some proper blues"'[23] as he tossed in leitmotifs that alternated Oriental-sounding exotica with hackneyed clichés of show-biz cabaret. Beck was to join The Yardbirds after Eric Clapton, uneasy about his colleagues' increasingly commercial outlook, transferred to John Mayall's Bluesbreakers, who'd opined that The Yardbirds were 'appalling'.[24]

Mike Cooper thought the same about The Pretty Things. 'Don't be misled by the same', he wrote in his diary after catching them at the 100 Club on 28 February 1964. 'This group are all atrocious musicians.'

Their origins lay in the Bricklayers' Arms auditions organised by Brian Jones – and involving Cooper – in 1962. Conflicting emotions at the Stones' unforeseen ascent into the hit parade had prompted Dick Taylor, in the more comfortable role of lead guitarist, to form the group in September 1963 with fellow student Phil May on lead vocals. Trainee insurance clerk Brian Pendleton's splendid amplifier was the deciding factor when he answered the pair's *Melody Maker* small ad for a rhythm guitarist to anchor Taylor's attractively rough-hewn solos and riffs. Pendleton was also required to pluck bass whenever the usual player, John Stax, doubled on harmonica.

With a temporary drummer, the Things made their public debut at the Central College of Art with Heath Robinson equipment and May's microphone fed through a jukebox. They paid further dues in December, with 'an eight-hour stint at the Royal Academy', shuddered Phil. 'When I came offstage, I had blood coming up from my throat.' Early fans included Malcolm McLaren and punk Methuselah Charlie Harper, awaiting respective distant destinies as The Sex Pistols' manager and fronting The UK Subs.

The Things' abandoned performances and extra-long long hair held instant appeal for record-company moguls looking for an act to combat the Stones. With Taylor's connection to those very Stones as useful in negotiation as a demo of 'Route 66', the Things were signed to the Fontana label after completing only their fourth paid booking.

Brian Jones kept what might have been a benevolent eye on The Pretty Things. In turn, they'd provide a safe house for him after Linda Lawrence, just before the Stones set off on a second British tour on 6 January 1964, announced that she was expecting a child – her first, his third – that summer. She seemed to intimate that her parents trusted that Brian would not decline the honour of their daughter's hand in marriage.

8 Don't Talk To Him

'He did something that was unnecessary from my point of view – and I also felt that it was a betrayal. I was in the same situation as a wild animal being hurt: it either attacks or runs.'

– *Pat Andrews*

We never see the man. We only see his art. Therefore, even if Brian Jones was still alive, how could we ever know if he was merely unlucky, cursed even – or if he was a sexual thug who made his women pregnant to bind them to him, shake up their complacency, or out of sheer bloody-mindedness? Was it a taking-to-heart of 'I Got My Brand On You', the opening track of *Muddy Waters At Newport*?

This latest blow wasn't exactly water off a duck's back to Brian, but before Linda's waters broke in June he was preoccupied with The Rolling Stones' harrying of the Top 10 with a third single, 'Not Fade Away', and then going all the way up with 'It's All Over Now'. An EP and, incredibly, an eponymous first LP would also warrant positions in the singles chart.

More important to Jones than Linda and the coming baby, too, were new complications of personal alliances within the group. The Edith Grove coterie was no more. Mick and Keith had found a less shabby flat near Willesden Green – and just about big enough for Andrew Loog Oldham to move in as well. Not so handy for West End nightclubbing, however, was the Lawrence family home in Windsor, where Brian was made very welcome and treated as though he belonged there to the extent of renaming the place 'Rolling Stone'.

However odd a choice this pop musician (and presumptive son-in-law) might have seemed for their Linda on first encounter, he doled out measured *soupçons* of charm to Mrs and Mrs Lawrence and Carole, the younger sister. Despite outward appearances, this Brian Jones was a gentleman, and quite famous, too, they told their neighbours. Yet, for all their growing familiarity with him, there'd be sudden lulls in the conversation, and that split-second look that mingled awe and scepticism – as if he wasn't quite real. No one told him why to his face, or mentioned any of the stories they'd heard about him.

The Lawrences couldn't have been more hospitable. They understood, for example, that Brian would rise late for a dressing-gowned breakfast. This wasn't only because of the Dracula hours of his onstage profession. Half-feeling her way down to the kitchen in the grey of morning, Mrs Lawrence would notice a crack of electric light under his bedroom door. Inside, Brian would be surrounded by smeared coffee cups, twisted cigarette butts and pages full of notation as, red-eyed and unshaven, he endeavoured to figure out a chord sequence to a fragment of melody that had come to him during a stroll to the newsagents that afternoon. Yet it was rare that a sketchy chorus, a ghost of a first verse or even a title satisfied a quality-control peculiar to himself as the one-man tunesmith, lyricist and arranger struggled to create just one number that would be suitable for the Stones – or anyone. 'Brian made some desperate attempts to write songs,' sniggered Ian Stewart, ' but they *were* desperate.'[1]

Theoretically, Brian's formal training put him a cut above Jagger and Richards, who had had to dah-dah 'head' arrangements to each other after Oldham's nagging had incited them to give this composing lark a whirl. Unlike Jones, they were, however, unencumbered by the same ingrained do's and don'ts that, traditionally, affect creative flow. The first Jagger-Richards A-side, 'The Last Time', wasn't quite a year away when they placed one of their efforts, 'Tell Me', on the group's LP, otherwise a 12-track streamlining of the stage act apart from 'Little By Little' (knocked together with help from visiting US producer Phil Spector) and 'Now I've Got A Witness (Like Uncle Phil And Uncle Gene)', a 12-bar instrumental with Brian extemporisng on harmonica over a riff borrowed from Tommy Tucker's just-released 'Hi-Heel Sneakers' as that of 'Stoned', flip side of 'I Wanna Be Your Man', had been from Booker T And The MGs' 'Green Onions'.

These and future output of this nature were attributed to either 'Phelge' or, more commonly, 'Nanker-Phelge', a corporate name for items to which all members of the group contributed.[2] These weren't just throwaway, either. 'Play With Fire', 'Off The Hook' and 'The Spider And The Fly', all inspired and solidly *bona fide* songs, would be born of Nanker and Phelge slinging in rhymes, rhythmic ideas, bits of tune and further twists to the plot when standing over, say, Brian or Bill at the piano as Charlie slapped a rhythm on a table, or watching Keith and Mick pacing up and down, bedevilled with an impulse that might have manifested itself at some inconvenient moment on their travels.

The 'Uncle Gene' of Nanker-Phelge's small beginning was Gene Pitney, one of the few North American singing stars to almost invariably make the UK charts during what would be remembered as the British Beat Boom, esteemed as he was for his stylistic consistency – 'squareness', some would say. Yet Pitney became a confidant of the Stones, deputising on piano for Ian Stewart on the album and, at Andrew Oldham's request, spending a long evening trying to tease workable songs from Brian, who had got no further than talking about what his head hadn't yet formulated in simple terms.

'There was nothing there,' reported Gene the next day, thus providing Keith and Mick with an excuse supported by authority, to cease taking Brian seriously as a composer.[3] Of Brian's lost pop songs, all that remains is a rather precious lyric (touching on 'the lashing tail of paranoiac fears' and 'the maniacal choirs that screamed out a warning') entitled 'Thank You For Being There'.

As for the melodies, Jagger thought 'Brian always made his songs too complicated... One hundred chords a minute like a jazz progression.'[4] This provided ammunition for Pat Andrews' defence that 'no one he knew had the ability to play his songs, including the Stones. He also wrote lyrics – though he'd call them poetry.'

Furthermore, for all his noted criticisms of Brian's 'too complicated' offerings, Jagger would confess later to have never heard a Jones opus from start to finish. He and Richards weren't very receptive to the work of other members of the group anyway 'so it was quite hard to know if Brian really wanted to do songs with us that he'd written', sighed Mick.

'I think he did, but he was very shy, and found it rather hard to lay it down to us – and we didn't try to bring it out of him.'[5] Keith Richards' corroboration was blunter: 'As far as I know, Brian Jones never wrote a single finished song in his life. He wrote bits and pieces. No doubt he spent hours, weeks, working on things, but his paranoia was so great he could never bring himself to present them to us.'[6]

Andrew Oldham, nonetheless, had persisted a little longer than Richards and Jagger with Brian, in case Gene Pitney's judgement hadn't been entirely correct. Perhaps Brian's forte was instrumentals. After all, 'Now I've Got A Witness' had been mostly his brainchild. What's more, he'd fallen in with Jet Harris after the former bass guitarist of The Shadows and drummer Tony Meehan had appeared with the Stones in *Southern Sounds '63* at New Brighton's Tower Ballroom. Jet and Brian's amity, however, might have been founded not so much on music as kindred spirits finding each other. Tidy-minded – or lazy – journalists could draw parallels. In The Shadows, Jet (or Terry, as Brian knew him) had been blond, albeit dyed, when the others were dark. They also found him 'difficult'.

Like Jones, he was promiscuous, later revealing to a Shadows biographer that 'I made five appearances there [a London VD clinic], and in the end they gave me a membership card. I'm probably immune to penicillin now.'[7] However, Cliff Richard's affair with Jet's first wife was 'another excuse for me to have a drink. It was bloody hard standing up on stage every night behind Cliff, thinking that he was having it off with Carol. I couldn't really stand the pressure, so I started drinking fairly heavily until it became a state of mind.'[7]

It had been a bittersweet 1963 for the gifted if self-destructive Jet. Shortly before accepting a music press award as 'Britain's top instrumentalist' at a Savoy hotel luncheon, he was badly injured when his chauffeur-driven Humber collided with a bus. As a consequence, his boozing – and intake of amphetamines – increased, and were central to a disastrous stage comeback in 1964, when he was so out of it that he introduced his backing combo, The Innocents, four times before stopping during the opening chords of his latest single, 'Big Bad Bass', and stumbling into the wings.

When he met Brian Jones, Harris was fresh from his first court appearance for being drunk and disorderly. A booker's risk and an alcoholic, he would have been the proverbial 'bad influence' if Brian himself hadn't been accelerating down the slippery slope already, via an increasingly immoderate consumption of favoured tipple.[8] 'Brian had a tendency to hang around with people who were out on the edge,' surmised Dick Taylor. 'He was already plumbing the depths then, out of his head a lot of the time.'

Of the same pop vintage as Jet Harris was Vince Taylor, a singer from Hounslow, with whom Jones also struck up a fast friendship. Taylor had had everything it took to be a second Gene Vincent until one unhinged evening at the Paris Olympia when he floated onstage in white vestments, rather than his customary biker leathers, to preach a repent-ye-your-sins sermon to a mystified and then furious yé-yé audience.

Vince, Brian – and Jimmy Phelge – were also omnipresent for a while at the Knightsbridge mews house of Hollywood jack-of-all-trades Kim Fowley and PJ Proby, an expatriate Texan with a magnificent, if mannered, vocal style and an outrageous public demeanour that was to climax in 1965, when his too-tight trousers split from knee to crotch during the second house at Luton Ritz. 'We had a non-stop river of naked women and rock 'n' roll crooks and geniuses,' laughed Fowley, 'and it was great times. We had lots of visitors including Brian. We had a cat there, and he stole it from us. Proby and I chased him down the street, and retrieved our cat – which he'd put up his shirt.'[9]

To entertain Jet Harris as much as the other unseen millions, Brian was to don black horn-rims for a take-off of Hank Marvin just after the commercials on a Stones *Ready Steady Go* special – and, on 3 May 1964, the *NME* reported that Harris was going to record a tune penned by Jones and Andrew Oldham. Three weeks later, readers weren't sure whether to believe the same newspaper with its, 'Brian Jones is likely to record a single on his own next month.'[10]

In the company of Terry Harris and others united by a taste for liquor, Brian had appeared to believe it absolutely when holding forth with a whisky and Coke close at hand to surreptitiously scribbling news hounds in the Pickwick, Speakeasy or Bag O' Nails, three of about ten fashionable London clubs from which pop conquistadors could select a night out.

Learning about these extra-mural projects only when information about them appeared in print, his fellow Stones shrugged them off as nothing more than Brian shooting his mouth off as usual. After the non-events of the Jet Harris instrumental and Brian's solo single (if they ever existed), on top of that depressing session with Gene Pitney as well as Mick and Keith's amused indifference, Jones's explorations as a composer were no longer to come into the Rolling Stones equation, no matter how dogged his persistence. As a postscript, a negligible if unique Jones-Richards piece, 'Dust My Pyramids', half a minute of Elmore James-esque noodling, kicked off *Rhythm And Blues*, a series hosted by Alexis Korner for the BBC World Service (then known as the General Overseas Programme) in October 1964.

It had been Alexis who'd blazed the strangest symptom of R&B's new acceptability when he led the studio band on *Five O'Clock Club*. The memory of its glove-puppet compere, Pussy Cat Willum, introducing Korner's gritty rendition of 'See See Rider' isn't easy to forget. Before 1964 was out, too, The Kinks, Animals, Pretty Things, Yardbirds and Spencer Davis Group would all debut in a Top 50 that would also accommodate a single each by John Lee Hooker and Howlin' Wolf.

By November, Wolf's double-bass player would be heading the list by proxy as writer of the Stones' unrevised 'Little Red Rooster', whose blues pedigree could be traced through a version by Chicago soulman Sam Cooke in 1963 to The Griffin Brothers' US 'sepia' hit in 1951 to the first recording by Howlin' Wolf. Just as 'Not Fade Away' had been mostly at Keith's instigation, so 'Little Red Rooster' was Brian's, his most sincere salaam to the music that had opened his heart. The risk of putting out a slow blues as an A-side was confirmed when the new single was the cause of one of the most major discrepancies between the two principal national music journal charts, entering at Number 15 in *Melody Maker* and going directly to the top in the *NME*.

It nestled uneasily in a Top 20 peopled by the likes of Gene Pitney, Val Doonican and The Helmut Zacharias Orchestra, as well as the new breed of 'hairy monsters' that, via exposure on Radio Luxembourg, not to mention the newer pestilence of offshore pirate stations, were making it harder for the BBC to give the public the 'decent' music it ought to be enjoying.

Not helping either were the likes of Adam Faith who made a pragmatic switch from lightweight 'Someone Else's Baby' ditties to ersatz Merseybeat – as heard on 1963's Top 10 restorative, 'The First Time'. It now read 'Adam Faith with The Roulettes' on the record label, and over the next three years Adam and this two guitars-bass-drums unit were to prove a competent team both on disc and on the boards, via idiosyncratic plunderings of black R&B catalogues as well as an assertive 'I Wanna Be Your Man'.

Enough of the old Adam remained to satisfy the faithful, but – compelled to appear straight after the Stones on 1964's *NME* Poll Winners Concert spectacular at Wembley Empire Pool – Adam, ready to murder his own grandmother, built on his predecessors' foreplay and all but out-Jaggered Jagger. Was this the same young man who, in pantomime as Dick Whittington, had led a children's chorus through 'Lonely Pup In A Christmas Shop' as 1960 rolled into 1961?

Faith was still sufficiently level-headed to appreciate the pop star's essential frailty and to have been amused by, for instance, press articles debating whether Helen Shapiro had been 'A Has-Been At Sixteen'.[11] Now pundits were saying that, while The Beatles were set to be British show-business treasures, the Stones would never last.

Brian Jones, too, might have been alighting with unspoken but perverse and nit-picking hope on the remotest indication of his group's fall, pontificating in the *NME* that 'The Who now occupy the position that The Rolling Stones held. They are the only young group doing something new both visually and musically.'[12] Meeting that same periodical's Richard Green not really by chance, he'd seized the opportunity to stick a pin in 'It's All Over Now': 'I'm not that keen on the record. It's all right, but, I don't know…it's just something.'[13]

If it had flopped, perhaps the Stones would have needed him again. As it was, his confidence was being eroded daily as he was pushed slowly but surely further into the background, during the strengthening dominance of the Jagger-Richards-Oldham axis.

'Brian's leadership of the group was engineered away from him,' noticed Don Craine. 'When I walked in on one of their rehearsals at Studio 51 as early as 1963, Brian was definitely being edged out. The big huddle there was Mick, Keith and Andrew. No one was saying a word to Brian, who was looking seriously peeved. He was already starting to dislike the fact that Mick was getting the adulation – and vice versa. It complicated matters, and Andrew wanted to simplify the image. One front man worked better.'

Beset with dark nights of the ego, too, Mick noted with trepidation Brian's often successful endeavours to steal the limelight. Both onstage and before TV cameras, while Jagger was dancing about, all Jones had to do was lift his eyes from the guitar neck and emit a rare bashful grin to cause cow-eyed girls to squeal with ecstasy.

On a headlining UK tour that summer, efforts to draw one from him were especially frantic throughout two performances at the Odeon in Cheltenham on 10 September, the very day that the Stones had been voted the most popular British group in a *Melody Maker* readers' poll. Three 16-year-olds started the queue days before the box office opened. On the night, the streets surrounding the Odeon were closed to traffic as police, linked by walkie-talkies, coordinated the group's admittance into the building. Outside, an enterprising fellow with a pile of monochrome A3 photos of individual Stones did brisk business on the night as even many without tickets began milling round the Odeon's Art Deco entrance.

Pictures of Brian outsold those of any of the others and, before the lights dimmed for the Local Boy Made Good's latest 'home game', he posed backstage for the *Gloucestershire Echo* between sports-jacketed 'old band mates'[14] he hardly knew, namely Mick Bratby and Buck Jones of a still-functional Ramrods, who'd risen from the youth clubs to recent supports to The Merseybeats, The Hollies and Brian Poole. 'We were always on the threshold of greater things,' a middle-aged Buck Jones would reflect, 'but as semi-professionals, we had to consider our jobs. In the end, I had to make a decision between being an estate agent and carrying on with the group.'[14]

The overflowing show itself was pop hysteria at its most intense. Pandemonium greeted compere Don Spencer's attempts to keep order and announce The Mojos, Simon Scott, The Innocents (now *sans* Jet Harris) and further unhappy artists, as the howls and chants for the main attraction welled up to a pitch where you drowned in noise. Somehow, the already ear-splitting decibels climbed when the Stones sauntered on. Then the volume rose momentarily to its highest, as if they'd all sat on tin tacks, after Brian delayed entering the spotlight a calculated second or two after everyone else. It was he, too, who was the target of nearly all the jelly babies, toilet rolls inscribed with messages of undying love and further votive offerings that rained onto the stage. 'It was the only place where everyone would ignore the rest of us,' smiled Bill Wyman, 'and scream just for Brian.'[15]

Open-mouthed, but not screaming, were a seated Lewis and Louise Jones, lately the recipients of a disturbing letter – from Mr and Mrs Lawrence – about a grandchild of which they'd been previously unaware. Julian Brian had been born to Linda on 23 July 1964 when the father was at a Stones photo session at Regent Sound in Denmark Street.

That the boy's forename was the same as that of his half-brother seemed as much of a premeditated denial as John Lennon's very public dedication to his second wife, of 'In My Life', a love song to his first, in 1969. Was the naming of Julian Brian a burning of boats? A symbolic, though ultimately empty, pledge to Linda? She might have preferred an engagement ring. If the child had to be called after one of Brian's musical heroes, why not Elmore – or Chester or McKinley, the respective baptismal names of Howlin' Wolf and Muddy Waters?

Whatever inner debate had led to 'Julian Brian', who could begrudge Pat Andrews horrifying Jones – and Andrew Loog Oldham – by telling her sad tale to trashy Sunday newspapers and taking part in an edition concerning illegitimacy of *Man Alive*, a current affairs series on the BBC's new second TV channel? Two telling sentences in her talking-head interview were, 'He's got no feelings for anybody. He just uses people and throws them aside.'[16]

With the candour of middle age, Pat was to admit, 'I would have kept quiet because I felt it was nobody else's business, but then Linda had this child – which was fair enough, but what hurt me was that they'd called him Julian. Instantly, I thought Brian was getting back at me, but why?

The last time we'd parted, there was no animosity. Without stopping to think about it, I went straight to the newspapers. Then Georgio Gomelsky suggested I should find a solicitor to help get some money for Mark. After a lot of messing about, the Stones organisation made me an offer of X pounds per week on condition that I sign a contract promising never again to speak about Mark in connection with Brian. I refused and set a paternity order in motion.'

Though there'd never be further direct contact with Pat, Brian was to speak to Richard Hattrell on the telephone after hearing that his pal had been poleaxed – like Pat the previous year – with peritonitis. 'I'd been advised to change my lifestyle,' recounted Richard, 'and I became a cocktail bartender. However, after I came out of hospital, Brian used to ring me practically every day asking me to re-enlist as road manager. He even got Keith to ring once to try and persuade me to come back. My father would pick up the phone on occasions and get quite cross with Brian.'

The calls came not from Windsor, but within earshot of central London's unremitting churn of traffic. Like the Andrews family before them, Mr and Mrs Lawrence had discovered that Brian Jones was not a gentleman – but maybe he'd never been one in the first place. To Linda's sorrow, he had packed his belongings and, through furtive negotiation involving Jimmy Phelge, had ensconced himself in the basement beneath the communal home of The Pretty Things in Belgravia.

'13 Chester Street' had been the title of an instrumental that used up needle time on the Things' first LP, rush-released in the aftershock of Phil May's cascading, girlish tresses, the longest male hair in the kingdom, flickering across a surly, blemished complexion on *Top Of The Pops* as the group – now with a permanent drummer in the alarming Viv Prince, another of PJ Proby's Knightsbridge crowd – mimed to their biggest smash, autumn 1964's 'Don't Bring Me Down', in the Top 10 at the same time as 'Little Red Rooster'. Rising almost as high, the 'Honey I Need' follow-up lived in a careering chord cycle thrashed behind May's ranted vocal. Punk or what?

This marked a period when the Things and the Stones were, arguably, on terms of fluctuating equality as belligerently unkempt degenerates detested by adults, to the purported extent of Andrew Oldham issuing a directive that the rival group was not to be rebooked on *Ready Steady Go* upon pain of the Stones boycotting the series. Even The Beatles were seen as a lesser threat when one more fat year for the Things began with chart strikes for 'Cry To Me' – also recorded by the Stones – and then self-penned 'Midnight To Six Man'.

In living at 13 Chester Street, therefore, Brian was in effect 'sleeping with the enemy', to use Phil May's playful expression, although outside the context of work the two groups were actually on friendly, even intimate, terms. 'Brian used to cry on my shoulder,' confided May, 'and say that he'd written this really good song, but that Mick and Keith didn't want to know. You could understand their attitude, because none of Brian's songs were suitable for the Stones. We'd tell him this, and he'd get angry and trash our records when we went out. He'd melt them by putting them near a lamp, and write insulting remarks about us on the mirror. He'd boast, too, about getting more fan mail than Mick and Keith. He was very uncool, very irritating, but I liked him.'

That Brian no longer held the Stones in the palm of his hand – or was even an equal partner – manifested itself in the way the others had started to behave towards him. Phil was privy to an incident when Brian was being driven to an engagement in Portsmouth by the stepson of the landlord. An overcharging alternator brought the vehicle to a halt between Guildford and Petersfield. Anticipating the Automobile Association patrolman's shaking head, Brian hailed the Stones' van, which happened to be passing 20 minutes later, but it nosed past, the passengers flicking vulgar signs at their gaping and stranded colleague.

The business over his – now discontinued – larger cut of concert income was one of many grievances against Brian, unconscious victim of intensifying character assassinations over venomous pints in a pub's murkiest corner. Furthermore, a couple of fellow Stones were just as appalled as Julian Brian's maternal grandparents over Brian's callous parting from Linda, and his sly, manipulative conduct towards girlfriends in general. The other four members of the group, therefore, were quite willing to cut off their noses to spite their faces by mounting the stage at Portsmouth without one who would be missed both musically and visually.[17]

His dignity twisted into a frown on the grass verge, Brian suffered alternate attacks of fist-biting anger and a peculiarly anodyne despair before reeling into the dressing room, hot, bothered and with a fresh zit erupting on his chin, after crumpling banknotes into the hand of a painfully slow taxi driver. How could they have been so nasty? How could they? Assurances that it was just an extreme bit of fun were belied by the inadvertent malevolence in certain pairs of eyes. Quickly dulling the pain by chemical means, Brian tuned up and then roamed the backstage area like a fakir in a trance, getting in the way and tripping over cables.

He poured his heart out to Phil May when the two quaffed a quiet Scotch and Coke together in Freddie Mills's, the Starlite Rooms 'and these rather strange clubs that were patronised by a mixture of leftish stars and gangsters – and CID flying squad, funnily enough', said May. 'People like the Krays were drawn to us because, if they were Public Enemy Number One, us and the Stones were Number Two.'

So it was that the *News Of The World* – one of the papers that had seized upon the Pat Andrews story – sent a couple of hacks to brave what they hoped would be the Edith Grove-like *demimonde* of 13 Chester Street which, even worse (or better), was a freeholding of the Duke of Westminster. Yet if doorstepping press visualised aristocratic portraits gazing down reproachfully on a tip occupied by depraved layabouts, they were to be disillusioned. 'They came round when Viv and I were having afternoon tea,' chuckled Dick Taylor. 'You could eat off the floor there.' Besides, neither Brian nor the Things spent much time there anyhow. 'It was only a crash pad,' explained May, 'as we were working nine days a week. We'd get back at five in the morning and leave at noon.'

On 16 April 1964, the day the Stones' first album was issued, the five had appeared at a riotous optimum moment – after The St Louis Checks and David John And The Mood – at the inaugural evening of Rochdale's Cubikclub. The Pretty Things, meanwhile, were booked to do likewise at St Andrew's Hall in Norwich, prompting a belated *Midland Beat* headline 'R and B Ousts Rock in East Anglia'.[18]

As the Things bothered the Stones, the Stones bothered The Beatles more. At the Liverpool premiere in July of *A Hard Day's Night*, the northern outfit's first movie, master of ceremonies David Jacobs had popped in a couple of *bons mots* at the expense of the Stones. For weeks, the film's title theme by The Beatles and 'It's All Over Now' had monopolised the first two positions in Britain's hit parade, necessitating the avoidance of such revenue-draining clashes in future.

There'd been plenty of Merseybeat acts at the *NME* Poll Winners Concert, but – The Beatles and The Hollies apart – none were able to take the Top 20 for granted any more. Interest was fading even on Merseyside itself, as epitomised by Liverpool lass Eileen Lawton's letter to *Mersey Beat*, complaining that all local groups sounded the same, so much so that 'I am now a fan of The Rolling Stones. Mick, Brian, Bill, Charlie and Keith are all individualists in their own right, and they make their contemporaries look insipid.'[19]

9 Golden Lights

'Brian's fringe was enviably straight. He must have only just taken the Sellotape off.'
      – Alison Evans at Chester Royalty Theatre, 1964[1]

On 26 July 1964 The Downliners Sect had been one of the supports at the Alexandra Palace, The Rolling Stones' first domestic concert after returning from a maiden tour of the USA three days earlier. Perhaps it was because the Stones weren't quite back to Greenwich Mean Time yet that 'they kept themselves to themselves', noticed Don Craine when passing the time of day with them along backstage passages.

Jetting back to London, Brian had wrestled with occupational as well as personal stocktaking. The Great Adventure had been, he considered, a qualified success. Long before the Stones had landed at Kennedy Airport on 1 June, the US media had emphasised their notoriety to such a pitch that adolescent North America and its exploiters had anticipated a freak carnival of greater magnitude than even The Beatles and The Dave Clark Five, whose visits earlier in the year had precipitated what has passed into myth as the 'British Invasion'.

Yet, whereas The Beatles had been greeted by the unison banshee scream they'd mistaken for engine noise on touchdown, the Stones' welcome was relatively muted, mainly because, unlike John, Paul, George and Ringo, the way hadn't been paved by a Number One in *Billboard*'s Hot 100. Thus far, the Stones' progress in that same chart had been negligible. 'Come On' had not been deemed worthy of a US release, and 'I Wanna Be Your Man' had B-sided 'Not Fade Away', which was creeping around the lower reaches of the Hot 100.

A few hundred fans converged, nevertheless, on the airport's upper terraces as the newcomers faced long corridors of light and shadow; cameras clicking like typewriters, and stick mics thrust towards their mouths in hopes that they'd crack back at the banal, ill-informed and damned impertinent questions – mostly about whether they were wearing wigs – with a Beatle-esque combination of zaniness, unsentimentality, unblinking self-assurance and the poker-faced what-are-you-laughing-at way they told 'em. Coming across as more rivals to The Dave Clark Five than The Beatles, nothing particularly funny or even significant emerged from the Stones' lips, either then or during the first jet-lagged radio interview – on New York's WINS station – an episode of wryly deadpan shallowness conducted by a yapping presenter with the *nom de turntable* of Murray the K.

From Manhattan's Astor Hotel, Brian dared a stroll around Times Square on the afternoon prior to an internal flight to Los Angeles for a mismatching on a television variety show hosted by Dean Martin, one of Frank Sinatra's back-slapping Rat Pack, who dished out derogatory quips at the Stones' expense. Next up was a US concert debut in San Bernandino on a bill with Bobby Vee, Bobby Goldsboro and Bobby Comstock, blow-waved human digests of stolid all-American dictums – your parents' word was law, don't talk dirty, etc.

Generally, the remaining shows were either like that or poorly attended headlining affairs such as Minneapolis's half-empty Excelsior State Ballroom, though all's well that ends well, and during the last dates – two shows compered by Murray the K at Carnegie Hall, no less – capacity crowds went crazy enough to provoke a ban on pop extravaganzas there for the foreseeable future. Moreover, a US-only single of 'Tell Me' was inching into the national Top 30 – which meant that the rapid follow-up, 'It's All Over Now', would be guaranteed a fair hearing.

The highlight of the trip, however, wasn't public. 'It's All Over Now' was taped in Chicago, which was like a Desperate Dan cartoon in its contradiction of familiar mystery. A Woolworths reared up in North Clark Street, scene of the St Valentine's Day Massacre, Coca-Cola tasted just the same and pizza was the Windy City's answer to fish and chips. Yet the sights and sounds in the streets – the ones the Stones were able to experience – were so diverting that they could be hours ambling just a kilometre or two to Chess Studios, 2120 South Michigan Avenue.

'I'd go back there tomorrow just to do some straight session work,'[2] said Brian of the studio where Chicago blues lived as pungently and as pragmatically as it did in the down-and-out State Street busker lilting an unaccompanied and never-ending 'Hoochie Coochie Man' as if optimistic of sexual congress, possibly on the very pavement. Inside Chess, Brian, perhaps more than anyone, was putty in the hands of the same house team that had forged the definitive works of Waters, Wolf, Diddley and Berry. Indeed, the venerated Muddy chanced to be present when the Stones were working on his downbeat 'I Can't Be Satisfied'.

Their revival featured what Brian was to cite as 'one of the best guitar solos I've ever managed'.[3] Yet, while it was selected for *The Rolling Stones No.2*, a UK album chart-topper, it didn't appear on its US counterpart, 1965's *The Rolling Stones Now!*. This was because North American LPs tend to include fewer tracks, but why was 'I Can't Be Satisfied' one of the omissions? Jagger and Richards' 'What A Shame' could have gone without any hardship.

Such an affront, however unintentional, fuelled Brian's growing paranoia about how dispensable a Stone he was. When the group returned to North America in October, he had been afflicted with a stimulant-related complaint so grave that it required intravenous feeding during a four-day stay in a Chicago hospital. 'His ego took a terrible battering,' said Johnny Dean, publisher of *The Rolling Stones Monthly*, 'when he missed several gigs because he was ill, and nobody noticed.'[4]

Quite what Dean meant by 'nobody' isn't certain, because in particular territories Jones rather than Jagger was The Man. Somewhere in vast stadium audiences as amorphous as frog spawn lurked many a musician who Brian was to outfit with musical – and visual – personality. These had crawled from the US subcultural woodwork as respective players in legion Anglophile 'garage bands' who'd been able to grow out their crew cuts and seize upon whatever aspects of the 'Invasion' idioms they felt most comfortable. While Lowell George – who first attempted bottleneck through Brian's inspiration – was one of The Standells, a Los Angeles outfit, it was Jones's straight 'pageboy' hairstyle, fringed to the eyebrows, as much as his instrumental skills that captured the imaginations of two of The Byrds, Bryan Maclean of Love and most of ? And The Mysterions, outfits built to last as 1960s pop legends.

Less renowned examples abounded in every region of North America. Typical were Toronto's Ugly Ducklings, whose 1966 single, 'Nothin'', sounded more uncannily like the Stones on the radio than too many similar offerings by too many lookalikes who'd also mushroomed on the crest of a craze with the right image at the wrong time – and in the wrong place. The twin peaks of the Ducklings' short career would be extensive local airplay for 'Nothin'', and opening for the Stones at Toronto's Maple Leaf Gardens. Crucially, they were fronted by a vocalist who looked like someone who looked like Brian Jones. A year earlier, he had probably gazed with yearning at the sleeve of *The Rolling Stones Now!*.

Though being like Brian had become so ultimate an objective for such exquisites, it was less fun for the lad himself for reasons connected with the gnawing away of his self-worth as a musician – at least while he remained somewhere in the Stones' ill-defined hierarchy, between Ian Stewart's road crew and the high command of Jagger, Oldham, Richards and, I suppose, Eric Easton.

There were, nonetheless, episodes akin to a schoolyard situation in which a child teased mercilessly through the autumn term is suddenly popular when his playmates return to class after Christmas – a sense of, 'Brian has been tormented quite enough. Let's start being nice to him.' Mick spared an unknowing Brian the worry of another paternity suit by helping Andrew Oldham draft a letter to the aggrieved lady in question, settling the matter. Keith, especially, could be less covertly protective towards Brian, once lashing out with his boot at a youth close enough to have spat at Jones when the Stones appeared before a heaving mob of 9,000 in Blackpool's Winter Gardens in June 1964 – a show that ended in a shambles of broken chairs, an up-ended grand piano and smithereens of drum kit and guitar amplifiers.

Yet Richards sided with Oldham and Jagger over the issue of who was and wasn't allowed to sing onstage. 'Brian could sing,' thundered Pat Andrews, 'but he was informed he wasn't to do backing vocals any more. They more or less told him that he was rubbish at it.' The issue, however, may have had less to do with the quality of Jones's light baritone that, if lacking individuality, had hitherto been loud and tuneful enough to harmonise and engage in call-and-response with Mick, most conspicuously on 'Walkin' The Dog', the debut album's finale (which also embraced Jones's appositely piercing whistle). 'Brian was supposed to be doing that,' perceived Dave Berry during a two-week UK tour with the group in 1965, 'but he kept shying away from the microphone – which annoyed the others.'

Reduced to moaning ineffectually about such slights – and there were plenty more to come – the timid songbird sought tawdry compensation after a fashion by pulling birds on a grander scale than ever before, and stressing his 'fear' of marriage in interviews. This was motivated, too, by resentment of Jagger's image as the group's principal sex symbol, and delight at the quicksilver front man's continued irritation when Jones stoked up screams by just standing there. Offstage competition also raged over the favours of female artists on any given tour – and Brian seemed to be winning.

Twinkle was the only one on the bill during a brief trip to Ireland in January 1965. She'll always be remembered for 1964's Decca single, 'Terry', a death disc concerning a biker, who, irked by his girl's infidelity, zoomed off to a moonlit end of mangled chrome and blood-splattered kerbstones. His legacy is a lifetime's contrition for Twinkle, until she – bent and wizened – totters up to the gates of heaven, where, it would be pleasant to imagine, he is waiting for her.

From car windows, Lynn Annette Ripley – called 'Twinkle' almost from her birth in 1948 – had noticed but never spoken to rough boys like Terry, or fake ones like The Rolling Stones, during a sheltered infancy and private education at Kensington's Queen's Gate School that she rather endured than enjoyed. Other former students included daughters of the Redgrave acting dynasty and Camilla Parker-Bowles, the Prince of Wales's future *paramour*. She knew few less wealthy than her own people in refined Kingston Hill, sometimes London, but preferably Surrey.

'Terry' was within an ace of Number One, and a follow-up, 'Golden Lights', being readied for release, when Twinkle descended on Belfast with the Stones for the opening bash at the ABC Theatre. 'I was just 16, experience nil,' she recollected, 'and I danced up and down on the stage in my leather gear, not really thinking of anything, and mouthing in a vacuum, but I could feel the crowd warming to me by the time my backing group played the opening bars of "Terry". Afterwards, the lights went down, and I fled to the wings. Someone grabbed my arm. "You were lovely. Well done!" I looked up into the eyes of Brian Jones, and our eyes met and held.

'The compere could not hold the crowd back any longer: "And here they are, the ones you've all been waiting for, the fabulous Rolling Stones!" Brian touched my cheek, then ran past me onto the stage.

'Back at the hotel after the final show – in Cork two days later – we talked of ghosts and strange happenings far into the morning hours. Mick grew tired and went to bed, and gradually the others followed. Only Brian and I remained.

'The next morning, we boarded the plane for London, and Brian and I automatically sat in adjoining seats. Mick came over and said furiously, "Move over, Brian. I'm sitting next to Twink." Brian turned and said softly, "I think the lady has made her choice." Mick wandered off moodily to another seat and never approached me again, but it was the start of a warm friendship between Brian and I that was to last for some months. I'd been the only girl on the tour, and they'd both wanted to go out with me, and spend the night with me, I suppose. During the flight, I felt sick and Brian held the paper bag over my nose.'

Brian's tilting for the downfall of Twinkle's knickers was frustrated, but other up-and-coming starlets were too willing to bed useful men who, dispensing sex almost out of politeness, might further their careers. Further paternity claims, justified and otherwise, emphasised Brian's appeal in this respect.

Many of his women, however, weren't mere gold-diggers. One of my interviewees, a now middle-aged lady of leisure from New York who prefers not to be named, recounted spending time with Jones at Chester Street that belied for the most part his reputation as a love-'em-and-leave-'em hoochie-coochie-man: 'My friend Delores had met him during a Stones tour of the States, and it was her who made the introduction in a bar along King's Road. I kissed him on the cheek, a familiar experience for him: a reasonably attractive female assuming an instant intimacy on the strength of his fame.

'Perhaps thinking he'd got lucky, he invited us back to his flat. It was all very 1960s bohemian when he led us inside. Delores was put to work in the kitchen to make coffee, and I was dragged into the bedroom, where the carpet was strewn with clothes. Within a minute, I was fighting off Brian's routine attempt at seduction. I didn't care who he was: it was all very presumptuous on first acquaintance!

'His endeavours were nipped in the bud further by the arrival of someone from the Stones office to oversee a *Music Echo* interview with a restive Brian about a new single, "The Last Time".

'Yet, he was cordial enough, I guess, giving "good copy", but I felt sorry for him, and didn't feel able to leave when everyone else did. After a while, I couldn't anyway because I discovered that the front door was locked with no sign of a key. He'd trapped me, but I suppose I could have made enough fuss for him to let me out. However, I saw a lonely soul, the real person behind the myth, and I responded more readily to this than I had to the guy who'd tried to make out with me a few hours earlier.

'So it was that I lingered for the rest of the night and into the next day. With the record player on in the background, we recharged our wine glasses at regular intervals, and spoke of many things – his surprising liking for Shostakovich, for example, and then his description of the Rolls-Royce Silver Cloud he was thinking of buying from George Harrison. Next, he insisted on ringing a guy in Cheltenham, and getting me to talk to him.

'When I awoke around noon, he was gone, and a glaring blonde woman – probably one of his bedmates – was standing over me. I made the proverbial excuses and left. Besides, I had to attend to my visiting mother on her first trip to England. Nevertheless, I couldn't wait to see Brian again – and when I did, his flat was impressively cleaner and tidier. He was composing on the guitar but, flatteringly, he broke off to greet me. Why had I taken so long to come round again? To my explanation about Mom, he replied: "Well, she didn't see London if she didn't see me!" What would she have made of him?

'Understanding my directionless personal situation, Brian wasted no time in asking me to move in – in short, to be his girlfriend. An instinct told me that this would be a terrible mistake. I'd end up as an adjunct to Brian Jones, my identity lost in his and the hoopla surrounding it. Why did he desire any permanent arrangement with the likes of me?

'I feel that I was privileged to know him when his guard was down during the days and nights that were left to us. Among cherished moments were Brian and Brian Pendleton [of The Pretty Things] improvising round a blues. Had I died and gone to heaven? Then there was Brian [Jones] composing again – and sounding me out about what notes he ought to play next. Why ask me?!

'I decided my time was up when he didn't want me to go on a forthcoming British tour with him. Of course, it wasn't as final as it should have been, because I went to one of the concerts – in Guildford – and experienced him with the Stones just like any other member of the audience. Yet there were few pangs of regret, and I remain happy to have seen Brian Jones in a different light, and for the memories of one of the most extraordinary experiences of my life.'

The garments observed scattered on the bedroom floor were symptomatic of Jones channelling much of his creative energy into being the best-looking member of the group – indeed, of *any* group. Becoming a Beau Brummell *des jours*, he adhered to Mod conformity from late 1964, ordering suits made to measure with a discreet correctness so uttermost that they would have earned praise for a smart turnout at Matins from the vicar of St Mary's. Everything had to be just so: back vents precisely seven inches (18cm) one week, five (12.5cm) the next. How wide are lapels now? The jacket covered either rollnecked nylon pullover, or a shirt with a tie inclined to be plain or patterned rather than Op Art. He never forgave himself when an *NME* journalist remarked in print that 'unbrushed shoes spoilt Brian's entire smart appearance',[5] though his conscience wasn't pricked to any discernible depth when he stole Brian Pendleton's striped matelot's jersey to wear on *Ready Steady Go*, a TV appearance that caused it to become a wanted fashion accessory.

The poet Henry Thoreau reminds us, 'When a soldier is hit by a cannonball, rags are as becoming as purple.' No matter how fine a figure he cut, Brian could find no remedy for his atrophied position in the Stones. Before 1965 was out, strange news would fly up and down that he had approached Paul Jones, Eric Clapton, Jet Harris and Viv Prince with a view to forming a new group.

10 It's Not Unusual

'He probably felt that Keith was doing loads of guitar parts – so Brian got carried along with all the experimentation that was going on then.'

– Dick Taylor

If the rumour had substance – or even if it hadn't, but Brian had started it – it was regarded as a registered protest rather than boat-burning. Nevertheless, none of the other Stones thought to plead or remonstrate with pop's most prominent and malcontented supporting player, though Ian Stewart called at Chester Street with a reminder about the following week's recording session at Olympic Studios.

If Brian Pendleton could be persuaded to transfer to bass, Brian was well placed to have filled a vacancy in The Pretty Things, as John Stax had just emigrated to Australia. Dick, Phil *et al*, however, tended not to have hits any more. Yet, in the metropolis at least, it was still cool for everyone who was anybody to call at 13 Chester Street – although some socialites and middle-aged trendsetters behaved like Victorian gentlefolk visiting the Elephant Man's bedsit in the London Hospital, torn between the sordid thrill of being out of bounds and a desire to flee the place, never to go there again. There has always been a certain *épater la bourgeoisie* about hanging around with social pariahs, and describing to toffee-nosed friends what happened in detail just to watch revulsion chase across their faces.

Marathon vigils by starstruck loiterers outside Belgravia's most concentrated target for graffiti were rewarded, therefore, when chauffeur-driven vehicles disgorged A-list celebrities of the calibre of Lionel Bart,

Diana Dors and Rudolf Nureyev. 'Judy Garland also used to come to our flat a bit,' reminisced Phil May, 'probably because she and Viv Prince had a mutual interest in the bottle. Viv invited me to a double date with him, Judy and someone for me – who turned out to be Rudolf Nureyev. So we danced the night away, Judy with her dress over her head and no drawers on, Rudy holding my hand. He was big news then, as he'd defected only about three weeks before, and it was like having a Martian on your arm. He danced like a Woodentop, too. He couldn't even order a drink then. The barmen in the Ad-Lib didn't speak much Russian.

'All I remember of Judy is her gripping my wrist in her claw-like hand. As she spoke, I could see blood coming from under her nails as they dug into my skin, but it seemed impolite to pull my hand away.'

Invited back for coffee, Garland, an international entertainer well into her 40s and near the end of a badly frayed tether, put her head round Brian's door. Now exiled in Britain by US tax demands, she was heading towards a fatal overdose of sleeping tablets, but a month at the prestigious Talk of the Town was a virtual sell-out. Brian plus one would be on the guest list when Judy sang before faces and cleavages tanned on the ski slopes, bow-tied tuxedos, pearly adornments and drinks like melted crayons that had paid to let a show-biz legend seize possession of them.

As far away from Elmore James and Howlin' Wolf as he could be, Jones snapped mickey-taking fingers to a big band keeping studio-smooth pace as Judy tore it up with 'Alexander's Ragtime Band', 'Johnny One Note' and the opening 'Get Happy', and evoked an agreeably blue mood with, say, her 'Over The Rainbow' signature tune, reprised as an encore.

Well, it was a laugh, and it pleased egocentric Judy that a Rolling Stone – one of her entourage had to remind her which one it was – had shown interest. It was also something big to tell his parents, who'd be more impressed that he knew Judy Garland than Bob Dylan – who dropped by Chester Street during his first major UK tour and was to namecheck The Pretty Things in 'Tombstone Blues' on his 1965 album, *Highway 61 Revisited*. Dylan was particularly friendly with Brian Pendleton, who conducted him downstairs to meet the other Brian.

Dylan and Jones had a mutual acquaintance in Long John Baldry – on whose floor Dylan had slept in December 1962 when in London to take part in a television play, *Nightmare On Elm Street*. A foreseeable bond soon tightened, too, between the Stone and one who, in 1959, had abandoned his studies at the state university in Minneapolis to take his chances in Greenwich Village, New York's vibrant beatnik district, where the civil rights movement would fuse with folk song to be labelled 'protest'.

As well as downhome intonation, untutored phrasing and eccentric breath control, Dylan had an idiosyncratic way with a mouth organ, was a fair acoustic guitarist and there'd been no complaints from Jones either about the intrinsic content of his first albums, which collectively embraced semi-traditional material as well as impromptu 'talking blues' and more earnest Dylan originals such as 'Blowing In The Wind', 'Masters Of War,' 'A Pawn In Their Game' and like comments on topical and sociopolitical matters that were outlined less skilfully by Phil Ochs, Tom Paxton and fellow mainstream folk intellectuals.

Though they'd hailed him at 1963's Newport Folk Festival, many Dylan enthusiasts had been disturbed by the lyrics of 'My Back Pages' and other items on *Another Side Of Bob Dylan* – which seemed to reject earlier profundities as strained and naive, and included a higher percentage of personal statements. He was thought to have 'sold out' altogether on the transitional *Bringing It All Back Home,* with its opening 'Subterranean Homesick Blues', for instance, lifting salient points from Chuck Berry's 'Too Much Monkey Business'.

Discernible, too, was Dylan's captivation with British beat groups and their US imitators, who had reciprocated by dipping into his songbook. Off-the-cuff examples are The Animals with 'Baby Let Me Follow You Down' (retitled 'Baby Let Me Take You Home') and 'House Of The Rising Sun' (also from Dylan's debut LP), Them ('It's All Over Now Baby Blue') and, most spectacularly, The Byrds, on whose million-selling 'Mr Tambourine Man' The Pretty Things had had first refusal.

It was also in the repertoire of The Walker Brothers – a trio from Los Angeles, just arrived to stake claims in the UK's musical diggings – and Nico, star of 1963's *Striptease*, a continental movie that preceded a spell as a model in Paris and Rome before landing a role in Fellini's *La Dolce Vita*. She also gained a recording contract, largely on the strength of her long blonde hair, high cheekbones and icy hauteur – oh, and a riveting German-accented contralto.

In 1965, she crossed the Channel for a slot on *Ready Steady Go*, singing 'Mr Tambourine Man' plus 'I'm Not Saying', a one-shot single on Andrew Loog Oldham's Immediate, the country's most successful independent record label of the 1960s. Thus Nico came to be associated by affinity to The Rolling Stones and, eventually, linked romantically with Brian Jones before and after she'd left to seek a bigger fortune in New York.

Among previous boyfriends was Bob Dylan, who penned 'I'll Keep It With Mine' with Nico in mind. He was courted, too, for further unreleased compositions such as 'If You Gotta Go Go Now,' a British Number One in 1965 for Manfred Mann (who, Dylan opined, were the most effective interpreters of his songs). The hunt was also up for a British Dylan, the job going initially to a denizen of the folk clubs named Donovan, who, with harmonica harness and nasal inflection, began on *Ready Steady Go* as a more beatific edition of the master.[1]

Outraged purists heckled when, sporting a solid-body Stratocaster, Dylan took the stage at Newport with The Paul Butterfield Blues Band – and undertook his 1965 tour of Britain with The Hawks, who used to back Canadian rock 'n' roller Ronnie Hawkins. Dylan's more openly commercial strategies were applauded, crucially, by John Lennon, whose newer songs – especially 'I'm A Loser' from 1964's *Beatles For Sale* – betrayed an absorption of Dylan through constant replay of his albums.

The Beatles attended Dylan's Royal Albert Hall concert, and his photograph was taken every time he negotiated the circular door of the Savoy Hotel. 'It was awe-inspiring to see girls screaming and trying to climb into his limo,' remembered Dana Gillespie, only a 16-year-old fan herself at the time. 'Every night the Stones and Beatles would come to the Savoy to play him their latest recordings. Everyone was in awe of Dylan, and he was the one person the Stones and Beatles had great admiration for. When he held court in one of those hotel rooms, everyone sat and listened.'[2]

Somehow, Julie Grant wormed her way into the charmed circle also, as did Donovan and Alan Price, late of The Animals. Furthermore, Dylan was captured on film busking the latest chart-busters by Dave Berry and, sardonically, Herman's Hermits. It was whispered, too, that he and Brian Jones had formed a desultory songwriting team, and that Bob had offered Brian the post of harmonica player in The Hawks.

Hard fact was that, on 6 November 1965, midway through the Stones' next US tour, Jones, Dylan and a retinue that included Al Kooper, organist on Bob's most recent single, 'Positively Fourth Street', spent an evening in New York, adrenaline pumping and talking shop constantly, in various nightclubs prior to looking in at a studio where soul shouter Wilson Pickett was recording possible follow-ups to his 'In The Midnight Hour' *magnum opus*. Later that same week, a power cut necessitated candles when Dylan and Robbie Robertson, The Hawks' guitarist, came to Brian's room at the Lincoln Square Motor Inn, a stone's throw from Central Park, to make music and discuss future get-togethers. Before he flew home this time, Brian was also treated as an equal by the late Richard Farina, a respected Irish-American 'protest' singer, who presented his new-found friend with a vintage dulcimer, a medieval stringed instrument, struck with hand-held hammers.

In Britain, too, Jones was admired as both a 'regular guy' and a multifaceted musician on a par with Steve Winwood, Manfred Mann's Mike Vickers, Alan Blakely of The Tremeloes and, at ease playing sax and keyboards simultaneously, Graham Bond. Within minutes of returning from a long tour of another continent, Brian had answered the knock of Winwood plus The Spencer Davis Group's nominal leader and road crew. Emotionally insecure as he was, Brian overvalued the goodwill of the more revered of his peers – even those still struggling. Banishing sleep, he made them welcome in his way: 'man, you should see the stuff we've got through,'[3] he boasted hours later, indicating the marijuana 'roaches' and empty bottles among the album sleeves, half-eaten food and stoned hangers-on littering the place.

'I remember Brian as being funny, sensitive, smart – with a slightly affected and fake upper-class intonation,' added Dave Davies, The Kinks' lead guitarist; 'a little pretentious, and very camp. I liked him a lot.'[4]

'Yes, but you don't know him,' Ian Stewart might have muttered darkly whenever he caught similarly affectionate remarks. 'Brian actually set out to be as stupid as he could,' grimaced Stewart, 'and as soon as he got any real inkling of money and success, he just went mad.'[5]

A more specific bone of contention for Ian was that 'all he wanted to do was dabble at other instruments. He hardly touched the guitar.'[5] Though Jones seldom missed opportunities to jam, he settled for piano rather than guitar, even if he relinquished it to Ian occasionally – as he did after hours in a Richmond pub with Dave Berry on vocals and one of The Cruisers on harmonica. By mid-1966, Brian was playing six different instruments during the course of any given concert.

In the studio, Keith Richards noticed, too, that 'Brian gradually gave up all interest in the guitar. He just wouldn't touch it – so it was down to me to lay down all the guitar tracks while he would be leaping about on the dulcimer or the marimba.'[6] Over the next three years, Jones was to weave all manner of quaint instrumentation into the fabric of Rolling Stones records, never more so than for 1966's *Aftermath*, reckoned by many – I, for one – to be the group's most inventive and original collection. During those sessions on which he was present, Brian would never again work so fully according to his considerable capacities.

The dulcimer on Tudor-flavoured 'Lady Jane' was of greatest antiquity, but marimba carried 'Under My Thumb' and 'Out Of Time', and the riff on 'Mother's Little Helper' was thrummed on a sitar, which Brian, messing about, had treated it as if it were some fancy guitar with its nine strings, movable frets and vibrating under-strings.

George Harrison had stumbled upon one among props accumulated for *Help!*, The Beatles' second feature film. Yet, while its wiry jangle was imposed on a track from *Rubber Soul*, both The Kinks and The Yardbirds had already invested respective singles with an Indian feel. Indeed, a seated sitarist had also been present at The Yardbirds session – for the hit single 'Heart Full Of Soul' – but the group preferred the more exotic twang of Jeff Beck. A deeper breath of the Orient would be exhaled by the Stones, courtesy of Brian's masterful sitar *obbligato* appearing on their third British Number One, 'Paint It Black'.[7] To more subtle effect, his sitar was to reappear on 1968's 'Street Fighting Man'.

Was there no end to this man's talent? Brian's tamboura was to fairy-dust 'Street Fighting Man'. Two years earlier, there was more marimba on 'Yesterday's Papers', flute on 'All Sold Out', sitar on 'Cool, Calm And Collected', trombone on 'Something Happened To Me Yesterday' – and his piano accordion had brought a mordant Jacques Brel-esque Belgitude to 'Backstreet Girl'. All these tracks were from *Between The Buttons*, marking time between *Aftermath* and 1967's psychedelic *Their Satanic Majesties Request*, on which Brian plucked harp, blew flute and saxophone and, on the *pièce de resistance*, '2,000 Light Years From Home', fingered 'a big old Mellotron,' said engineer George Chkiantz, 'with a delay between the moment you pressed a note and achieving a sound'.[8]

The hum of a faulty organ would mark, likewise, 'There's Always Work', a John Mayall instrumental, and an eerie vocal tremolo would make The Hollies' 'Lullaby To Tim' seem as if there was fluff on the needle. The imposition of further unusual sounds onto the grid of common-or-garden guitars, bass and drums was very much in the air as the age of Aquarius loomed – though the harpsichord that The Ugly's [*sic*], a Birmingham outfit, tried to push to pop prominence on their sole *Ready Steady Go* slot, had also conveyed an olde-tyme flavour on Jimmie Rodgers' 'English Country Garden', a Top 10 entry back in 1962, while the autoharp of Pinkerton's (Assorted) Colours (and New York's Lovin' Spoonful) had been pre-empted by The Downliners Sect. Nevertheless The Who showcased John Entwistle's French horn on 'Disguises' and 'I'm A Boy', and The Hollies again got their Tony Hicks to pick electric banjo on 'Stop Stop Stop'.

A tape of marching feet from EMI's sound archives was grabbed by The Hollies as rhythm track for a 1966 LP track, 'Crusader', and The Small Faces filled their bladders when trying to tune a tumbler to A, and peeped a soccer referee's whistle on 'Understanding', one of their B-sides. A pot-pourri of polyrhythmic percussion supplemented Mick Wilson's drumming on Dave Dee, Dozy, Mick and Tich's 'Save Me' as Tich's Greek bouzouki had already on *risqué* 'Bend It!' A final example is that of a now-forgotten singer on *Five O'Clock Club*, swivelling his head from side to side at the microphone regularly enough to convince me that it was for a deliberate vocal effect.

Brian Jones should have been in his element then, but he was absenting himself from more and more record dates – including, apparently, that for

'(I Can't Get No) Satisfaction', a key aural artefact of the Swinging Sixties. Often, he added his musical icing just as the cake was baked, and spoke of it later without pride as he weighed up the easy money and unchallenging procurement of sexual gratification against being in what was, as far as he was concerned, as much of a hard-sell pop act as Herman's Hermits.

Frank Zappa, leader of The Mothers Of Invention, would 'remember seeing Brian Jones very drunk at the Speakeasy one night, and telling him I liked *Between The Buttons*, and thought it superior to *Sgt Pepper*, whereupon he belched discreetly and turned around'.[9]

If partly self-inflicted, that Jones was increasingly less integrated into the main creative process aggravated a sense of isolation and bolstered what was now a fixed idea that his sole purpose as a Stone was to gild Mick and Keith's patterns of chords and rhymes. It was now beyond him to come up with one solitary composition of his own, let alone one, maybe two, per album, as John Entwistle did for The Who, Dave Davies for The Kinks or George Harrison, junior partner in The Beatles.

'Brian's only solution became clinging onto either Mick or me,' shrugged Keith Richards, 'which created a triangle of sorts. It was, like, Brian's open wound. Eventually, though, he became a sort of laughing stock to the rest of the band.'[10]

Marianne Faithfull was to be as amused by 'Brian's phantom songs', the consequence of 'manic scribbling in notebooks followed by pages being ripped out. Recording, erasing, recording, erasing. Reels unspooling all over the floor, the offending tapes being hurled across the room.'[11] Yet, according to Marianne too, while 'Jagger-Richards' was the composing credit for 'Ruby Tuesday', a US chart-topper, 'it was really Brian and Keith's song. It began, as I recall, from a bluesy Elizabethan fragment Brian was fiddling with in the studio. Brian in his sheepish way very softly played a folkish, nursery rhyme melody on the recorder. It was nothing more than a wispy tune, but it caught Keith's attention. Brian said it was a hybrid of Thomas Dowland's "Air On The Late Lord Essex" [*sic*] and a Skip James blues.'[12]

'Ruby Tuesday' was among four songs that Jagger sang under sufferance on ITV's *Sunday Night At The London Palladium*, broadcast straight after the prescribed hour of religious programmes on 22 January

1967. That he did so over pre-recorded backing, to which the others mimed, invoked howls of derision in the national press. Worse, at the end, the Stones refused to join the rest of the cast – which included a comedian, acrobats, a formation dancing team, Julie Grant and compere Jimmy Tarbuck – when they lined up to wave a cheery goodbye on the Palladium's revolving stage while the pit orchestra sightread the show's 'Startime' theme tune.

A couple of newspapers reminded readers of the previous summer when, via a private prosecution by a local youth-club organiser and the manager of an East London petrol station, Jones, Jagger and Bill Wyman were fined for 'insulting behaviour' – that is, urinating against a wall of the said garage and not taking steps to 'conceal this act'.

On the same tour, Dave Berry was in the convoy of cars from which the three desperate men had spilled: 'The pissing in the forecourt was blown out of all proportion of what it was. A *Daily Mail* journalist was travelling with us, and it was his job to find stories – like us, say, getting refused entry to a nightclub in Scarborough, things like that. He'd be straight on the phone as soon as the doorman said, "I'm sorry. You can't come in." We'd get chucked out of hotels, too – because, at the time, they weren't geared up to young pop musicians staying in them. Once we were working at a theatre in Manchester on a Sunday, and because the Stones and I were each wearing make-up, the manager brought the curtain down because make-up meant that it was a theatre production – which wasn't allowed on the Sabbath.'

Yet, even after the unpleasantness at the Palladium, the British public seemed to have got over the initial shock of The Rolling Stones, even accepting them as not a pop group as transient and gimmicky as any other, but a tolerable part of the national furniture like Promenade Concerts, ITV's *Coronation Street*, BBC's *Till Death Us Do Part* and The Beatles. They were even worthy of a modicum of grudging respect as stubborn eccentrics who would not 'go show biz'. Even fork-brandishing fathers disparaging them in breakfast rooms could differentiate between individuals other than Mick Jagger. Future *Times* correspondent Jonathan Meades' dad nicknamed Brian Jones 'Mrs Wormold' after a *cor blimey* sitcom character played by Patricia Hayes.

In retrospect, you could see the resemblance, particularly after Jones took to wearing floppy, wide-brimmed hats that were a little bit *femme*. See, elegance these days no longer meant invisibility. On *Top Of The Pops*, PJ Proby set a precedent by lip-synching his hit xerox of 'Maria' from *West Side Story* in buckled shoes and a batwinged blouson like whipped cream, while, also in 1965, the sub-Proby Beau Brummell, Esquire on *Ready Steady Go*, bowed from the waist over resident compere Cathy McGowan's hand during the introit to his flop 45, 'I Know Know Know', whilst attired just like his Georgian namesake.

Turning his back on Carnaby Street, no longer the be-all and end-all of menswear for such mods that still existed in 1966, Brian also scoured Portobello Road and Chelsea Antique Market, and made himself resplendent in olde-tyme lace ruffles, frock coats, costume jewellery pinning bandana-like cravats and trousers that, prior to dyeing, looked as if they'd once hung round the legs of an Edwardian matelot. Later, he'd experiment with dundreary whiskers and, briefly, a beard. As such he was ahead of like boutiques he'd patronise – notably I Was Lord Kitchener's Valet (which thrived during a craze later in 1966 for Victorian military uniforms) and the likes of Hung On You,[13] Granny Takes A Trip and other similar establishments that sprang up in London and the bigger cities, peddling Art Nouveau variants on old-tyme garb and imported Oriental exotica.

'Brian was an effeminate kind of guy,' confirmed Jim McCarty, 'but totally heterosexual. We used to share a girlfriend, Winona, in 1967. Brian's driver used to pick her up from my flat in Fulham.' What cannot be denied, however, is that Jones was as narcissistic as any Regency dandy, treating his appearance as a work of theatrical art, made afresh before he faced each day. To what extent may be discerned in remarks by Bobbie Korner after she saw Jones 'in that period of dressing up in eighteenth century clothes. We went to a concert and Brian came into a box above us, and I looked up at him and thought, "My God, he's gone. That isn't somebody dressing up, it's somebody who has disappeared."'[14]

Nevertheless, though Gene Vincent had been man enough for mascara, it was thanks to Brian that a hulking rock 'n' roller from the Gorbals or the Bowery now became more receptive to such a wardrobe, less who're-you-lookin'-at-pal defensive about wearing it down the pub, having come to know that no aspersions would be cast on his manhood. The impact was to spread over the decades. Just as the widest river can be traced to many converging trickles, so a source of glam-rock, New Romantic, Gothic and beyond must lie with Brian Jones.

His most jaw-dropping fashion statement, however, was the black jackbooted uniform of a World War II storm trooper in which he was front-paged – also grinning evilly and stamping on a doll – for *Stern*, a glossy magazine published in West Germany, a territory in which Jones was, debatably, still more idolised than Jagger. This was particularly inflammable in the light of a recent election triumph by the 'new Nazis' in Bavaria, not to mention a hastily withdrawn US album with a front illustration showing The Beatles as white-smocked butchers, hacking at bloody wares that also contained the limbs and heads of dolls. There was also a chronicled incident of The Who's Keith Moon, Vivian Stanshall of The Bonzo Dog Doo-Dah Band and Screaming Lord Sutch parading round London clubs in Nazi attire – though, after morning came, Sutch cried off when Moon sought further exhibitionist fun in one of the city's most Jewish quarters.

An *NME* interviewer noted a swastika flag draped over one of Jones's armchairs, but believed his protestations that the *Stern* picture was 'a put-down. Really, I mean with all that long hair in a Nazi uniform, couldn't people see it was a satirical thing?'[15]

It had been proposed by Brian's latest and, seemingly, very 'serious' girlfriend, 22-year-old Anita Pallenberg, whose background had parallels with Nico's as she, too, was a honey-blonde model and aspiring film actress. For a while, as long as Brian didn't mind her having distractions, too, his other amours could stay in the picture. A briefly reconciled Linda Lawrence was still there – just – and so was Winona, but in the foreground was Zou Zou, a French opposite number to Twiggy, Jean Shrimpton and others in the same mini-skirted league.

Brian was quite a catch for Zou Zou as, in France, the Stones were more popular than The Beatles, if behind incumbent luminaries Sylvie Vartan and her singing husband, Johnny Hallyday. Zou Zou's tastes ran to suggesting troilism with another of her lovers, Dave Davies, who, in a 1996 autobiography, also included the enigmatic sentence, 'Marianne Faithfull was Mick Jagger's girlfriend when she wasn't Brian Jones's girlfriend.'[4]

Others also detected a certain friskiness between Jones and Faithfull, who had become Jagger's after he'd finished with Chrissie, Jean Shrimpton's sister, and stopped pondering whether or not to try for a date with someone who was almost-but-not-quite as well heeled a pop star as himself – say Françoise Hardy or Dusty Springfield, though it was widely known that Dusty preferred women.

Despite suffering her first serious flop, Marianne was still a chart combatant in 1966. She was also sufficiently good-looking for Mick not to feel inferior to a proud Brian with his new 'bird' and, damn him, Anita – wasp waist, firm breasts, flawless complexion – was worth more than a second look. The attraction had been mutual from her first – well, it couldn't be described as a 'conversation' – with a vulnerable and alienated Brian backstage at Munich's Circus Krone on 14 September 1965. Tears weren't far away, following another of those flare-ups with one or more of the other Stones that had been growing more frequent of late. Dispensing with even perfunctory chivalry, but without a tang of lasciviousness, he'd asked Anita point-blank to spend the night with him: 'I can't be alone.'[16]

It did not begin, however, with an ecstasy of bodice-ripping. 'He needed someone to comfort him,' said Anita. 'I held him in my arms, and he couldn't stop crying – like he'd been holding back this pain and now he was able to let it go.'[16]

Like a marijuana 'joint', sex was proffered as a gesture of free-spirited friendliness, and Anita tagged along with Brian to the next Stones engagement in Berlin, where she discovered herself shivering with pleasure at the famous demure smiles he flashed at her from the stage. Her reaction was not lost on Brian, who had been impressed by a disarming self-sufficiency and a well read aestheticism that put him on his mettle, but would not permit him to be bothered by Anita's 'interesting' past. In any case, it would have been hypocritical of him not to have been morally generous about the fact that she'd hardly lived like a nun since her expulsion from a school on the other side of the city from the Circus Krone.

'He really liked me,' smiled Anita, 'and I responded to him. Basically, I moved in with Brian right away. He was very moody, which I like, and he was physically attractive as well. He looked like a girl in a funny kind of way. Sexually, I like girls as well as men, and Brian seemed to combine both sexes for me. Also, Brian was very outspoken, blunt, said everything on his mind, outrageous things, and he had a wonderful inquisitiveness – about new things, new places, everything that was going on. Except for Brian, all the Stones at that time were really suburban squares.'[16]

11 Silence Is Golden

'When I was a student, I lived at World's End in Chelsea, and used to see him staggering between Hung On You and Granny Takes A Trip, just down the road from my flat. He looked terrible, like some sort of dandy derelict.'

– *Jonathan Meades*

It would be Brian and Anita for 15 months before the fairy-tale went wrong. In the beginning, every day together cemented the two more securely in the same flow of feeling, and they crossed the impalpable barrier between implied companionship and hearsay of Anita telling her parents she wanted to marry the boy. A frightful row that could be heard all over the Scotch of St James was not an isolated occurrence, and other quarrels frothed and fumed behind closed doors, but Anita made Brian laugh a lot, and healed some areas of his wounded self-esteem. 'Brian was very short, especially his legs. He was a head shorter than I, and he could barely see over the steering wheel of his Rolls. He worried about the look of his teeth, which were capped, but I made him forget his defects, and just think about the positive side of Brian Jones.'[1]

He was centimetres taller through walking on air as he showed her off around the clubs. She read books and used long words – a lot of them in German, mind, but long words all the same. With beauty as well as brains, Anita Pallenberg was also just the sort of incredibly sexy blonde out of a foreign film – the pout, the giggle, the whole works – that teenage schoolboys would invent as a dream date when talking dirty.

Jones was in rhapsodies about how adventurous she was in bed, mention of which still brings out moonshine about what 'insiders' claim they heard and saw. Straight up. A mate of mine told me. Sado-masochism, coprophagy, Crowley-esque meddling with the dark arts and capsizing of assumptions that humans could only be gratified sexually without mechanical appliances and only with other humans – all were the least of it after Anita moved in with him.

Brian had left Chester Street when the bad name The Pretty Things were giving the place had set in motion the litigation necessary to flush out them and other tenants tarred with the same brush – an eviction held at bay by a *Checkpoint*-type television probe. For the past year, home for Jones had been Elm Park Road, between King's Road and Chelsea's second main thoroughfare, Fulham Road. Then he and Anita climbed a rung higher by purchasing a nearby but more up-market studio flat in 1 Courtfield Road, which, after they'd settled in, emitted a dimly lit aura of either cartoon scariness or fascinating depravity, depending on a given visitor's credulity. To Marianne Faithfull, it was 'a veritable witches' coven of decadent illuminati, rock princelings and hip nobility'.[2]

As Jagger-Richards A-side followed Jagger-Richards A-side, if Brian couldn't be the most dominant Stone he was going to be the most mystical one. Like Dean Moriarty in Jack Kerouac's *On The Road*, he'd be oddly fascinating for his mastery of an instinctive and crazed pagan Zen, radiated by the incongruous juxtaposition of Moroccan tapestries and a poster advertising Seven-Up on the walls of the new apartment, and his provocatively creepy face asking to be punched on the front sleeve of *Between The Buttons*.

The ancient Greeks had a word for it – *hubris*, which defies succinct translation, but alludes to a heroically foolish defiance rooted in a feeling that you are beyond the reaches of convention and authority. Brian had been trying to reach that plateau all his life. Now, in an adolescence extended by adulation, his hubris had been learned not through asceticism and self-denial, but via the dynamics of careless sex, psychedelics, the sub-criminality of his past and making it up as he went along.

At Courtfield Road, the mood of the hour might dictate a seance; a cosmic safari to some midnight tor 320km (200 miles) away in Cornwall to look for UFOs; 'Satanic spells to dispel thunder and lightning', as Winona reported to Jim McCarty; an excursion up west to Barry Miles's

Indica Gallery and Bookstore for merchandise of occult and modishly aerie-faerie nature and fireside palavers that swung from incorporeal matters to Brian's shy-making soliloquies about his life, his soul, his agony.

'He was a tortured personality,' discovered Anita, 'insecure as hell, totally paranoiac. He had a volatile temper, and he would react to frustration with physical violence. In his tantrums, he would throw things at me, whatever he could pick up – lamps, clocks, chairs, plates of food. Then, when the storm inside him died down, he'd feel guilty and beg me to forgive him.'[1]

Another method of staying his phantoms was through a drug more sinister than either the pills that had brightened the working week at Whiteley's or the short-lived magic of marijuana. Jones – with Keith Richards – first tried lysergic acid diethylamide 25 in December 1965. It had been 'turning on' factions within London's in-crowd for a year before it was outlawed for recreational purposes in 1966. Then, when questioned about LSD, Brian would insist in the first instance that, as far as he and the other clean-minded lads in the Stones were concerned, it still stood for pounds, shillings and pence.

The Pretty Things knew 'acid' well on the evidence of song titles like 'Trippin'' and just plain 'LSD'. Dick Taylor remembered that, 'The guys above my flat in Fulham were students who organised these lock-out nights – "raves", you'd call them now – at the Marquee, when acid was legal. Personally, I was extremely wary of it.'

'I had a good time on LSD,' countered Phil May, 'but other people had problems. In Germany, our lighting guy did the lights for the band that went on before us, thinking it was us.'

Known in the Middle Ages as 'St Anthony's Fire', LSD's paranormal sensations and surreal perceptions vary from person to person, from trip to trip. One psyche might boggle with nonsensical frenzy. For another, it could be akin to an extreme religious reverie or the start of a fantastic voyage to untold heights of creativity.

Too often for Brian Jones, he'd surface from a quagmire of horror. 'It's Anita's belief that Brian never recovered from his first trip,' reiterated Marianne Faithfull. 'Acid and pills only worsened his condition and compounded his paranoia into a full-blown persecution mania – but he embraced his horrors as if on acid he was able finally to confront his afflictions in a palpable form.'[3]

One evening at the Ad-Lib, he babbled his fears to John Lennon: 'They're destroying me. I started the fucking band, and now they keep trying to squeeze me out. It's all Jagger-Richards this, Jagger-Richards that. They won't even listen to my songs any more.' The arch-Beatle stared appraisingly and with not a little exasperation: 'Look, I get sick of Paul sometimes, of the way he's forever trying to dominate me. You have to stand up to these ego maniacs. You can't just get smashed out of your box. Look, how about if I ask you to play sax or something on some Beatles records? That'll make them all sit up and take notice, won't it?[4]

Gathering strength from this proposal, Brian progressed from joining in the *omnes fortissimo* chorus to 'Yellow Submarine' to honking woodwinds on two Beatles B-sides, 'Baby You're A Rich Man' and the knockabout 'You Know My Name'. Of Brian's hand in the latter, Paul McCartney commented, 'He was a really ropey sax player. He played a funny solo. It happened to be exactly what we wanted. Brian was very good like that.'[5]

By then, McCartney and Lennon were hearing less about Jones's own attempts at composing verse–chorus pop. His music had always been stronger than his songs. In an electronic den at Courtfield Road, he was more inclined to potter about with pieces of intellectual rather than aesthetic intent. Scant of lyric or melody, these had more to do with the pioneering tonalities of Varèse, Stockhausen and Cage than '(I Can't Get No) Satisfaction'. While spending 'an extremely pleasant evening' *chez* Jones that autumn, Keith Altham of the *NME* found his host 'enthusiastic, but embarrassed by his efforts. One tape was astoundingly effective with a weird, psalm-like chant going on in the background like an electrified Black Mass. Some further electronic experimentation sounded like The Who after a few drinks.'[6]

Expressions like 'cross-fade', 'white noise', 'tape loop' and 'square wave' – as well as words such as 'field', 'gate' and 'aperture' when applied to cine photography – pocked conversations with Dave Thomson, a film student Jones had met at Glasgow's Odeon Theatre during the

Stones' last UK tour. They were collaborating on a screenplay for an 'experimental' film not meant to 'go anywhere' any more than those you might see in installations at final exhibitions for Fine Art degrees at your local university.

It is not known whether the Jones-Thomson liaison was either vaguely if mostly head-scratchingly entertaining, or an antidote to pleasure on the principle that the more arduous the effort needed to appreciate it, the more 'artistic' it is. However, Brian's butterfly concentration alighted on another project for long enough to bring it to fruition.

After Anita had landed a leading role in a German film, *Mort Und Totschlag* (A Degree Of Murder), late in 1966, Brian – motivated perhaps by jealous imaginings – had materialised whenever possible on set in Munich, watching her act on a monitor screen, and monopolising her during the lengthy intervals as cumbersome movie cameras were repositioned. His omnipresence entered discussions by the flick's backers, aware both of its budget and the publicity value of a Rolling Stone's involvement.

Volker Schlondorff, the 27-year-old director, was elected to sound out Jones about composing the soundtrack. If flattered, Brian confessed that he hadn't a clue how to go about it, but rather than balk at the task like a gymkhana pony refusing a fence, he decided to muddle on with it, getting a clearer picture from the confusion, learning what he could *in situ* and unwittingly dismissing many ingrained preconceptions and introducing new ones. As if it was the most natural thing in the world, he was 'spotting' each sequence with a stopwatch, and returning to London to routine it at Courtfield Road before repairing to Olympic Studios to supervise the taping of music that was impressive in its own right, regardless of imagined visuals. Within its tight strictures, it was to testify to the presence of more intrinsic virtues than had been expected of one in an industry where sales figures are arbiters of success.

With a Deutschmark sign over every note, Brian himself attended to sitar, organ, dulcimer, banjo, harmonica and autoharp, but he also called the shots to a small ensemble hand-picked by himself and engineer Glyn Johns, among them guitarist Jimmy Page (now a Yardbird), Nicky Hopkins, one of Lord Sutch's Savages prior to choosing the more comfortable sphere of session work, and vocalist Peter Gosling of Moon's Train, a group co-produced by Bill Wyman.

Their blithe dedication to the job in hand was refreshing. Furthermore, they enjoyed being under Brian's surprisingly straightforward baton as, rather than sinking morbidly surreal teeth into *Mort Und Totschlag* and exploring an abstract unknown that needed to be explained rather than scored, he delved into C&W, blues, soul and what might be described as 'country and eastern' – though the lightweight main title theme was reprised in wracked, menacing fashion in keeping with the illicit burial of a corpse on the construction site of an autobahn. Elsewhere, a serene if subdued ghostliness vies with severe dissonance, but little was designed to divert attention from the action, which was precisely what Volker Schlondorff required: 'It wasn't just that his music was special. It was that the score was so spontaneous and vital. Only Brian could have done it. He had a tremendous feeling for the lyrical parts, and knew perfectly the recording and mixing techniques to achieve the best sound.'[7]

To Brian's chagrin, *Mort Und Totschlag* wouldn't be subtitled or dubbed and put on general circulation in Britain. Instead, it was the stuff of occasional showings in arts centres and film clubs. Neither was the soundtrack to be issued on vinyl. Therefore, while quite free with his opinions about the Vietnam war, persecution of homosexuals, the new Abortion Act, drugs and religion, he didn't touch on *Mort Und Totschlag* – and neither did Keith Altham mention it – when they met in a Kensington pub not long after the New Year got under way.

Keith Richards was hovering on the edge of this interview, as he had when Altham had visited Courtfield Road. It may not have been connected, but he'd been around Brian quite a lot since the advent of Anita. Though Brian had long lost hope of penetrating Keith and Mick's caste-within-a-caste, he loved these increasingly more frequent occasions when he had Keith's apparent solicitude and they were head to head over guitars like at Edith Grove, or fiddling about with avant-gardenings like the 'electrified Black Mass' to which Altham had listened the previous October.

Utterances unamusing to anyone else would have Richards and Jones howling with hilarity on the carpet, but in studio, aeroplane or tour bus with the Stones, Brian's concentration was split when his ears strained to catch the old murmured intrigue as Keith sided with Mick in the resumption of antipathy, sleights of verbal judo and further mind games. 'When The Yardbirds toured with the Stones and Ike and Tina Turner in 1966,' said Jim McCarty, 'I noticed that Mick and Keith weren't talking to Brian, and that they were pulling faces at him onstage.'

Still, the sunshine of Keith's smile and its reminder of 1962, when they'd truly been friends, was nice while it lasted. Having observed instances of Richards' hesitancy with regard to girls, there was, as yet, no reason for Brian to suspect ulterior motives as Anita 'got to know Keith quite well, and I was intrigued with his laid-back, taciturn nature – so different from Brian's aggressive personality.'[1] As for Richards, while he may have presumed that a 'suburban square' like himself was out of Pallenberg's league, there were long, dangerous moments between them whenever Brian was out of the room.

Anita and Brian were invited but were unable to attend a house party at Redlands, Keith's Sussex lodge, on that fateful February weekend when he and Mick were busted by a local narcotics squad, tipped off by the *News Of The World*, whom Jagger had spoken of suing for libel after an article connecting him to LSD had resulted from two of its reporters mistaking him for Brian, who'd obliged them by outlining his drug-taking career in unholier-than-thou fashion one night in a London club.

While awaiting trial, Jagger and Richards thought it best for the garrulous Jones to come, too, when they removed themselves to a faraway place where they wouldn't see police or journalists in the foliage. Mick and Marianne chose to fly, but, with Tom Keylock, a Stones' road manager at the wheel of Keith's Bentley, Courtfield Road was the starting-off point for the trip to Morocco – where Africa almost touches Spain – via France for Keith, Anita, Brian and a couple of monied hangers-on.

Brian had first been to Morocco during the Linda Lawrence era, but it was during a week's holiday with Anita in 1966 that the rhythm of the sun-scorched life there had got under his skin. When benighted in a settlement of the Joujouka, part of a nomadic tribe of the Rif foothills, he'd become engrossed in particular by themes from time immemorial investigated undynamically and at length around the oil lamps and hookahs by hand-drummers and exponents of high-pitched *rhaita* panpipes – which, it was said, could only be played by a true Joujouka.

As with LSD, one individual's reaction to the master musicians of Joujouka can be markedly different to that of another – some listeners are bored stiff, while others find them hypnotic – but they sent Brian into a sonic trance. Overwhelmed and excited by the experience, he understood why the natives revered their music as a force of, and inseparable from, nature, as much one of the eternal verities round which the seasons revolved as growth, death and rebirth. From the moment Brian heard it he was inescapably involved, and was torn between keeping quiet about his cultural secret, trying to superimpose it on the Stones' musical grid and spreading the word about it to the rest of the world.

He was certainly thinking aloud about Joujouka music to anyone who would listen during the drive through France that was not without incident. Towards the Mediterranean coast, Brian suffered an asthmatic seizure of such gravity that, wheezing like a bellows, he had to be half-led, half-carried from the car into a hospital near Toulouse where he was advised to stay overnight, at least. At his insistence, the journey to Morocco continued without him but, engulfed by eddying agitations connected with mistrust and attention-seeking during a second day of treatment, he asked a nurse to ring reception at the booked hotel in Barcelona, instructing Anita to double back to him.

Yet, flung together whenever Keylock took bends too fast, Pallenberg and Richards in the back seat were each cherishing a caprice to entice the other into bed. Initially, it was no-strings frivolity, but nevertheless for four days Anita shrugged off both Brian's telephoned message and consequent telegrams.

If now able to tread the corridors without aid, the man walking towards Anita with his arms out had every appearance of being seriously ill, and the African idyll was put on ice so that Jones could jet back to London for tests and to recuperate further. Naturally, the person the papers referred to as his 'constant companion' had to accompany him.

Counselled to avoid stressful situations for a while, a holiday in sunnier climes in congenial company seemed appropriate. In Morocco, however, tension was in the air, and Brian guessed from tacit signals during an excruciating first day round the hotel pool that something had occurred between Keith and Anita.

With Brian's illusions about her now dead, a façade of self-composure was maintained in public, and he and the other male in the triangle remained on terms that were in turns civil and aloof. It was infinitely easier to give Anita a hard time than Keith. However, hours of unnerving histrionics and noisome home truths in the bedroom culminated not in Brian's defeatist bunch of fives striking Anita – although they certainly did – but in his return from a search for vicious amusement in the local bazaar. Looking streetwalking prostitutes up and down like a farmer at a cattle auction, he selected two girls to bring back in order to fuck them, one after the other, in front of an enchanted or disgusted Anita. Either way, a vestige of some code of honour peculiar to himself would be satisfied.

More emotional scum rose to the surface: the whores performed their duties – or at least had been ready to do so – and were paid to go away. It had all gone awry, and Brian lost his temper. Everything went red as hell. He hit harder than ever before for the sake of himself, as roars of rage and distress gave way to grunting and heaving. The volcano had erupted to a life-threatening degree, and so he held Anita to him like a vice, panting and sobbing, and becoming aware of the trickling of blood.

The next day, Pallenberg's make-up couldn't quite mask the damage. Richards said nothing, but had had all he could stand of both Morocco and the 'fragile monster' that Jones had become.[8] It was time to go anyway as the press had ferreted out his and Mick's whereabouts, and tomorrow's curtain would be drawn to reveal a sea of faces and flashbulbs.

That afternoon, when Brian went souvenir hunting, Keith fled with Anita. In London two days later, they were holed up in a *pied-à-terre* he kept in St John's Wood.

For Brian, this was the Portsmouth trick 1,000 times over. He bottled up the pain on the next connecting flight to Heathrow, staring moodily at the clouds as twilight fell on both the continent beneath him and his disjointed thoughts. Eyes bloodshot with tears and fatigue, he went through the motions of storming round to the hideaway to confront a stone-faced Keith and plead with Anita, but an uglier showdown was defused when, with a kind of despairing triumph, it dawned on Brian within minutes that Anita would never cross the abyss that now lay between them.

Of course, he wouldn't have been the Brian Jones of bed-hopping legend if, when people asked, he hadn't made light of it, assuring them that he had tired of Anita Pallenberg long ago and had been on the verge of finishing with her. In the Speakeasy or Blaises, he'd throw back his head with laughter at some vulgar joke shared with Keith Richards, demonstrating to all the world that any bad blood between them had been diluted. Yet what was the point? The truth would out, and everyone would know that he had been cuckolded by Keith as surely as Keith had already wrestled the leadership of the Stones from him.

Shrouded in darkness and rumpled bedclothes at Courtfield Road, catharsis was followed by a dull ache. Careworn hours passed either in uneasy slumber or, nourished by fast food and worse, in front of the television.

Gradually, his rise from half-death became perceptible. He was spotted with John Lennon absorbing a Fourteen Hour Technicolor Dream at Alexandra Palace where the effects of LSD were emulated via the contrast of flickering strobes and ectoplasmic *son et lumière* projections on the cavernous walls as 'bands' (not 'groups' any more) played on and on and on. One after another, they 'did their things' on platforms erected at either end of the exhibition centre. As well as old pals like Alexis Korner, The Pretty Things and Graham Bond – some garbed in expedient kaftans, beads and like flower-power tat – the extravaganza featured the very top drawer of British psychedelic pop: Pink Floyd, Tomorrow, The Move, The Soft Machine, The Crazy World Of Arthur Brown, you name 'em.

Jones was most impressed by The Move, whose singer charged onstage with an axe to hack up effigies of notable world figures before turning his attention to imploding televisions. 'They are really an extension of the Stones' idea of smashing conventions,' he had remarked to Keith Altham. 'Destroying TV sets *et cetera* is all part of dissatisfaction with convention.'[9]

While Brian dug The Move, of all the new acts at large in London in 1967 he was particularly captivated by Jimi Hendrix, a psychedelic Wild

Man of Borneo who was frightening every guitarist in the audience with the scope and vision of his playing, with drummer Mitch Mitchell and, on bass, Noel Redding keeping nimble pace.

Dick Taylor remembered 'chatting to Jimi in some crowded dressing room as he tinkered on his Stratocaster – and I kept losing the thread of the conversation because he was just as amazing musically on an unamplified electric guitar as he was with one plugged into a 200-watt stack'. Hendrix was regarded then as having more in common with UK lead guitarists like Dick and Brian, whose solos and riffs were constructed to integrate with the melodic and lyrical intent of each song rather than the technical challenges of underlying chord sequences. Of the same persuasion were Dave Davies, Ian Amey ('Tich' in Dave Dee, Dozy, Beaky, Mick and Tich), Peter Green from John Mayall's Bluesbreakers – and Jeff Beck, who confessed that he 'just hadn't the guts to come out and do it so flamboyantly'.[10]

Flashier players such as Eric Clapton and The Who's Pete Townshend were stunned by the newcomer's display of eclecticism and unpredictability in compatible amounts. Like Brian Jones, the two of them reportedly went to every Jimi Hendrix Experience engagement in the capital prior to the trio's first assault on North America. So forceful was the publicity build-up that the Experience were billed above The Who, sitar virtuoso Ravi Shankar and even local lads The Grateful Dead, on 18 June during the International Pop Music Festival in Monterey, a few kilometres down the coast from the flower-power city of San Francisco, now as vital a pop mecca as Liverpool had been.

'Things weren't coming in half-measures,' crowed Noel Redding. 'I was flying first class to New York, seated next to Brian Jones, who had taken me under his wing.'[11] With Eric Burdon, another passenger on his way to Monterey, Jones underwent an LSD trip of such length and piquancy that, grinned Burdon, 'by the time we'd got to our hotel, Brian and I were about ten feet [3m] off the ground. After checking in, we managed to make it to the elevator – but neither of us made it out. We rode up and down for hours, laughing hysterically at each passenger who was unlucky enough to come through the doors and ride with us.'[12]

With the party on the internal flight was Nico, who, following a part in 1966's *Chelsea Girls*, Andy Warhol's most enduring movie, had been prominent in his mixed-media 'Exploding Plastic Inevitable' troupe as an adjunct to The Velvet Underground, whose perspectives on seedy-flash New York life had taken tangible form as literary-musical wit on a sensational debut LP that appealed to Brian Jones for its unprecedented coverage of drug addiction, sexual taboos and mental instability.

The group were precursors of a style so nebulous in scope that The Doors were cited by some as a Los Angeles variant of the blueprint. By coincidence – or not – Nico's latest conquest was Jim Morrison, The Doors' X-certificate rabble-rouser-in-chief, exploited as a cross between a modern Dionysus and a singing Marlon Brando. Echoing Brian's ruminations on The Move, Morrison liked 'ideas about the breaking away or overthrowing of established order. I am interested in anything about revolt, disorder, chaos, especially activity that has no meaning.'[13]

While Morrison hadn't yet pressed his hardest on the nerve of how far he could go, Jimi Hendrix's act was as staggering as it was ever going to get when, introduced at Monterey by Brian as 'the most exciting performer I've ever heard', he streamlined all the outrages that were old hat back in London: jackknifing into the air, practising fresh-air cunnilingus, gnawing his guitar strings, collapsing to his knees and, during the 'Wild Thing' finale, sacrificing his instrument in a pitiless *woomph* of lighter fuel.

Out of the spotlight, Jimi was a quiet, mild-mannered soul, strolling amongst the hippie multitudes with Nico and 'the young Prince Jones' of 'Monterey', a slice of musical journalism soon to be a US hit by Eric Burdon and his New Animals.[14] If sipping at an uncharismatic can of lager, Brian on that Saturday afternoon was like a squire on a walkabout at a village fête, his easy smile not resting on individuals but diffused to the general populace. He and Jimi were no ordinary sightseers, but there was no disruptive, clothes-tearing commotion as there might have been anywhere innocent of Californian *sang-froid*. 'He and Hendrix were just walking round, looking at the displays,' noted photographer Jim Marshall. 'Brian was, like, rock royalty and followed round by a load of people, just looking at their hero. The night before, he had seen Otis Redding close the show and absolutely destroy the place, and he made this great comment to me, "The Stones think we're the best band in the world, but you couldn't give me a million pounds to follow Otis."[15]

His old gregarious self again – or so it appeared – Jones was also sighted back in the London clubs, holding forth with a glass filled at regular intervals by one of a bevy of dolly little darlings. His bitter freedom had made him a celebrity jackpot for 'groupies' – once called 'scrubbers' – with raw physical beauty their only asset. Brian knew the type well and was wary. Nonetheless, the calculating lust for them was as strong as ever. However, while he was partial to variety, this latest library of fleeting attachments tended to shelve editions of the same woman.

Anita had had the decency, or work schedule, not to be around much during what turned out to be Brian's final tour with the Stones – a trek across nine countries in continental Europe with the associated and ceaseless harassment by customs officials who'd clocked in for work after reading about Keith and Mick's imminent court appearance, and had then treated them and the rest of these Rolling Stone scruff-bags in the same way. After every fibre of red tape – including a body search – that bureaucracy could gather had exacerbated his residual misery, Brian would slouch onto the boards to unacknowledged screams with a face like an Edith Grove winter, reacting instinctively as a tempo announcement pitched him into another Jagger-Richards number with a four-four backbeat that even a halfwit couldn't lose. Sometimes, banal ritual deferred to the ancient, almost extra-sensory jubilation, but then he'd catch sight of Keith with his crotch-level Stratocaster.

Exhausted and deeply depressed after this most harrowing public ordeal of his stage career, all Brian wanted to do was step aside from the fallout of Mick and Keith's trial. However, on 10 May, the very afternoon that they were remanded on bail, Courtfield Road was invaded by Scotland Yard officers, who had reason to believe that the premises were being used for the consumption of controlled drugs, contrary to the provision of the 1966 Dangerous Drugs Act, Section 42.

At four o'clock, the place still slept like the dead, and Brian met plain-clothes Sergeant Norman Pilcher's pounding at the door, with bare feet, budgerigar eyes, tousled hair, a kimono and the bewildered pallor of someone coming down from Norman knew not what. Flashing a search warrant and barging in, he aimed to find out as his men started in the panelled lounge, emptying the ashtrays into polythene bags. The ransacking concluded with Brian and the overnight occupant of the spare bedroom, a young Swiss aristocrat, being arrested for possession of grains of cannabis and minuscule quantities of harder stuff.

It had been, philosophised a fatalistic Jones, as inevitable as an oft-seen episode in the BBC's recent repeats of *Hancock's Half Hour*. It was almost as if he'd willed it to happen. An amateur psychologist might theorise that, by putting himself in the same agonised boat as Mick and Keith, he'd be a big wheel in the gang again. Alternatively, perhaps it was to beef up his bad-boy image. Whatever those two could do, he could do it worse.

Raw fact is that Brian had answered and ignored telephoned tip-offs of the impending intrusion, possibly from sympathetic journalists who'd been told themselves by contacts inside the force. At any rate, a photograph of Brian on the balcony of Courtfield Road during the actual raid was to be published in one tabloid, and a crush of further press was already obstructing the pavement outside Chelsea Police Station when Brian was escorted in for the formal charge.

That evening, he went to the cinema. Two days later, he shopped for clothes in Chelsea Antique Market. He'd escaped by the skin of his teeth too many times since Valerie and the adopted child to be unduly bothered by this latest spot of bother. After the trial date was fixed for 30 October, he bounced thoughts off a designated solicitor. Brian considered that the amount of drugs in question wasn't sufficient to justify making much of a fuss. How bad could it be? All right, so he'd be fined a couple of hundred quid, taking into account inflation. Maybe a conditional discharge as well? That had to be the limit.

The brief shook his head doubtfully. Judging by the atmosphere at the West Sussex Quarter Sessions where Jagger and Richards were in the dock, Jones could expect the stiffest possible penalty. There was, however, a small rise of hope when Mick and Keith's jail sentences were dismissed on appeal, triggering the rush-release in August of 'We Love You', a Stones single bracketed by topical prison-door sound effects. Yet Brian's puffed, slitted eyes in the promotional short told their own story. Those two were off the hook. He wasn't.

It would help, said his lawyers, if it could be argued that Brian needed psychiatric treatment rather than jail. As well as being frail and haggard from the arrest and the still-resurgent shock waves of Anita and Keith, who could regard him as 'normal' after so many years of being under pressures that John Citizen couldn't begin to understand? Taking this to heart, Jones got himself admitted to a residential clinic in rural London between Richmond and Kew. Set in 16 square kilometres (4,000 acres), it contained uniform magnolia-coloured single bedrooms that were frugal but bearable enough. The regime was, too. As well as sessions on the couch, inmates were subject to compulsory exercise, group therapy, confinement to the estate's boundaries and no sex.

In cold print, it reads like prison, but, from an unpromising beginning, the new patient reacted well to its order and discipline, and was able to re-encounter the outside world with his ways changed – or so both Jones and his counsel assured the bench. Neither this nor the defendant's neat pinstriped suit softened court chairman Robert Seaton's heart. Loudly, as if addressing a mass beyond the stained-glass windows of the Inner London Sessions, he spoke of pop stars setting an example to their admirers, and him failing in his duty if he didn't send Brian down for nine months.

12 Little Arrows

'The fact that a member of Brian's own group took Anita away, poisoned any possibility of the Stones ever functioning the way it had before. There was really no chance for Brian to survive in the group after that.'

– Marianne Faithfull[1]

It wasn't on the vast scale of the protests that followed the incarcerations of Jagger and Richards, but a demonstration that snowballed to 30 participants around Sloane Square in pouring rain was unruly enough to necessitate 12 arrests.

This exercise in futility made no difference as the hours dragged by for Jones in Wormwood Scrubs, where he had been issued with regulation ill-fitting garb with the texture of a horse blanket, and allocated a cell. Hanging over him like a Sword of Damocles was an enforced visit to the prison barber for the standard short back and sides with electric clippers. However, though Brian had reached the stage of half-hearted attempts to be pleasant to the guards and the other convicts, his belongings were returned to him and a thumb jerked at the cell's open door. A mere 20 minutes later, with all his hair still on his head, Brian Jones was free.

An expert appointed by a High Court judge had examined him and had been convinced that his mental state was precarious, even suicidal, and this had tipped the balance in favour of an appeal hearing on 12 December 1967. On the day, he appeared contrite, but his facial expression might have been more to do with a raging toothache. Nevertheless, the bench agreed that Brian had learned his lesson, and that he had every intention of staying out of trouble for the foreseeable future. He wasn't, therefore, to receive dental treatment back at the Scrubs, but pay a hefty fine and be put on probation for three years. His behaviour was to be monitored, too, via regular consultations with a psychiatrist.

Despite an implied promise that he'd never touch narcotics again, Brian, weak with relief, celebrated by getting smashed out of his brain almost immediately. A culmination of this escapade, his pulled molar, the eternal asthma and the general strain of that particular week brought about a collapse at Courtfield Road, his body vibrating with shuddering gasps and every pore on an ashen complexion bestowed with a pinprick of sweat. Contrary to medical advice, however, Brian discharged himself from hospital before there was a chance to instigate procedures to find anything in his bloodstream that might interest his probation officer.

Five months later,[2] Brian's resumption of his drug habits was in less secretive focus via another run-in with the law. This time, rather than respond to the relentless bell push – Sergeant Pilcher again – he dialled the Stones' office before the police gained forced access. When an aide's engine died outside, Brian's persecutors were belabouring him about some cannabis they'd uncovered in a ball of wool from the drawer of a desk.

'I don't knit. I don't darn socks. I don't have a girlfriend who darns socks,' he'd also plead when, after two nail-biting adjournments, the case came up on 26 September. This was true enough, but the jury still thought he was guilty as hell. Under the circumstances, Brian had no right to expect mercy, but those psychological problems of his proved helpful again, and he got away with a fine as inappreciable as the amount of dope with which he'd been caught – or he had had planted on him.

'Brian's main preoccupation then was a severe paranoia about being busted,' deduced Keith Richards. 'He had no other thoughts in his head except hiding from the police.'[3] For the proverbial 'moral support', Keith and (more often) Mick had been present at various of Brian's court appearances, and, in the weeks leading up to the last one, he was put up in Redlands, out of reach of Pilcher, the press and temptation.[4]

A conciliatory, even amicable mood persisted when he was in the studio, too, though Jones could no longer see Richards as even an inconstant pole of alliance. In any case, all the Stones were becoming quite accustomed now to life without Brian, who was present only if his rising from a bed of dreams induced by prescribed tranquillisers coincided with a remembered record date.

'He would turn up for sessions when he felt like it,' concurred Jimmy Miller, producer of the albums that followed *Satanic Majesties*. 'One night, he showed up after he hadn't bothered to come to the previous four. He had a sitar, and we were doing a blues song. It might have been "No Expectations". There was no way a sitar was going to fit, but I was happy that he was there. Mick and Keith, however, would come up to me and say, "Just tell him to fuck off. He hasn't been here for days", and I'd say, "Yeah, but the guy's got problems. Don't you think we have some responsibility to encourage him to show up, and not tell him to piss off when he does get here?" Their reply was, "You're new on the scene. We've been putting up with Brian's nonsense for the past two years."'[5]

Even Bill Wyman, the steady older man, had had his fill of Brian Jones: 'I never disliked him as a person, although he was a bastard sometimes, but I found it impossible to get on with him musically. You couldn't rely on him, but he wasn't unique in that he was messed up. A lot of people in bands were messed up then.'[6] Wyman gave an example: 'Brian's contribution to "You Can't Always Get What You Want" was to lie on his stomach most of the night, reading an article on botany.'[7]

Jimmy Miller was to praise Brian's slide playing on 1968's *Beggar's Banquet*, though Keith was now secure enough in his far primer position not only to plan to take a lead vocal on the next album, *Let It Bleed*, but also to cross another demarcation line by applying his coarser bottleneck wherever he felt appropriate.

Richards also played both bass and lead guitar on *Beggar's Banquet*'s most memorable track, 'Sympathy For The Devil'. Its making was documented in a film of the same name[8] by Jean-Luc Godard, who, though approaching his 40s, was regarded as an *enfant terrible* among movie directors. During long weeks of daily scrutiny of the accumulated celluloid miles, Godard noticed Jones asking Jagger, 'What can I play?' 'Good question,' was the cutting riposte. 'What can you play, Brian?'

While he joined in the 'oo-oooo' background chant, and was allowed to hack negligible chords on an acoustic guitar, Jones was reduced to just shaking maracas when, on 12 December 1968, 'Sympathy For The Devil' was the penultimate number in *The Rolling Stones' Rock 'N' Roll Circus*, a cancelled television spectacular that would gather dust for decades until it acquired historical interest.

Brian found the *Rock 'N' Roll Circus* as onerous as he had the Jean-Luc Godard project. As matters deteriorated more, he wished he was in hell rather than Olympic Studios for what would be *Let It Bleed* – well, maybe not hell, but Morocco for the week-long Rites of Pan Festival in Joujouka.

He'd already summoned up the emotional detachment to revisit the scene of that dreadful day when he'd breezed back to the hotel to find Anita and Keith gone. The following spring, less a holiday than a field trip – with Glyn Johns along for the technological donkey-work – had produced a net result of some tapes of the G'naou, a percussion-dependent ensemble, for purposes that were non-specific – though Brian would speak of grafting on backing tracks by those New York session players most capable of dissolving outlines between jazz and rock.

'Ethnic' music was in the air in 1968 – *on* the air, too. On the BBC's new Radio One, John Peel, the station's most cutting-edge presenter, had moved from inserting 20-minute ragas between progressive fare on his *Night Ride* programme to bowing to frequent requests for 'that boot-slapping thing' (Zulu step dancing), 'the Russian with the funny voice' (a singer from Azerbaijan, USSR) and further curiosities that he'd chosen from Broadcasting House's sound archives. A national pop station filling off-peak ether with nose flutes, Romanian cobzas and further outlandish examples of what would later be termed 'world music' had been unthinkable three years earlier, when Brian Jones's sitar had lacquered 'Paint It Black'.

The *nth* Womad festival that swelled the population of Reading for one weekend in July 2003 epitomised the continued impact of 'world music'. Although English remains the predominant language of pop, it's more feasible than ever before for both the US Hot 100 and *Top Of The Pops* to be infiltrated by acts from Iceland, France, Senegal, Spain, Japan – you name it – and among the first creaks of a door that would open wider on this treasury had been Brian Jones's musical safaris in Morocco.

His most fruitful expedition took place in August 1968, when George Chkiantz flew over at short notice to assist in the recording of Joujouka festival highlights. 'When Brian was in the mountains, he was splendid,' said George. 'He was attentive, and a great, considerate host.'[9] He was also an honoured guest of the tribespeople. Indeed, if not quite Spanish adventurer Francisco Pizarro amongst the Incas, the descent of a robed and golden-haired alien into their Joujouka midst left its mark in 'Brahim Jones', a ditty sung still by children of the village. Translated, the third of its five lines runs: 'He recorded our music for the entire world to hear'.

Between five and ten hours of Joujouka material was taken back to London for editing down to album length. Thrusting aside the G'naou notion of adding Western accompaniment 'it was decided to retain the original music,' explained Chkiantz, 'but also lend it a new dimension in the studio in order to make it an expression of the journey.'[9] Yet, though phasing and other studio effects were to pervade side one of 1970's posthumously released *Brian Jones Presents The Pipes Of Pan At Joujouka*, 'The 4,000 Year Old Rock & Roll Band'[10] was heard *au naturel* on side two.

For those compelled to buy everything on which The Rolling Stones so much as breathed, *The Pipes Of Pan At Joujouka* required effort. It wasn't remotely in the realms of pop, but some listened again – and again, and again – until it reached out and held them for ever. Nonetheless, perhaps because Brian was their *bête noire*, the other Stones didn't want to be keen on it, especially as Jones was flunking out of more group commitments than ever now, having distanced himself geographically from London by purchasing Cotchford Farm, a property in the Sussex Weald that, in a horrible way, was to be almost as synonymous with his name as that of a previous owner, the author AA Milne.

Since dwelling at Cotchford Farm in the 1920s, the late Milne's plays, novels and humorous newspaper articles have been forgotten, but his children's books remain popular, especially those with Winnie The Pooh, a toy bear, as the hero. Written for Milne's son, Christopher Robin, the second of these, *The House At Pooh Corner* – serialised in the *Sunday Express* in 1928 – was inspired by the ivy-clung mansion from the pages of *Country Life*.

After considering similarly secluded havens in Surrey, Hertfordshire and Essex, Brian had taken up residency at Cotchford Farm as rain and dull weather span out 1968's harvest into November. As its exposed oak rafters and stone-flagged floors attested, the house dated back to the Plantagenets, though the aqua-blue thermostatically heated swimming pool was constructed in 1964.[11] Nevertheless, only the odd aeroplane from Gatwick need remind the new owner of what was over the hills in London, where, shuttered underground in the clinic-cum-dosshouse paradox of the studio, his headphoned ears had felt like braised chops as he thrummed take after rejected take of 'Sympathy For The Devil'.

In the quietude and fresh air, he didn't yet miss the limelight as the seasons changed from gold to marble. As they did, the log fire in the living room subsided to glowing embers and, on the clear nights of early December, the moon in its starry canopy would shine as bright as day over the vastness of storybook meadows and woodlands. Brian would live long enough to see the landscape melt into another endless summer day with not a leaf stirring, a touch of mist on the sunset horizon and a bird chirruping somewhere.

He was out of earshot of the hastening conspiracy. Nearly all the cards were now on the table. The group couldn't carry him anymore, and Brian – now referring to 'they' rather than 'we' – couldn't envisage being a Stone for the rest of his days, and was bracing himself for a leap into the unknown.

About once a month from around the middle of 1966, the music papers had been reporting a schism in some group or other. After The Pretty Things bid a final farewell to the singles Top 50 with a cover of a Kinks LP track, 'House In The Country', the first to quit was Brian Pendleton. According to Phil May, 'We were on a train to Leeds – and when we got there, Brian was gone. He'd got off somewhere, so we struggled through the five or six dates we had in the north as a four-piece. When we got back to London, Dick went round to Brian's flat, and the door was swinging open like the *Marie-Celeste*. He had taken his wife and baby and just vanished.'

Pendleton's dramatic disappearance coincided with Manfred Mann taking formal leave of Paul Jones at the Marquee in October 1966. By then, Wayne Fontana had cast aside his Mindbenders while Georgie Fame had disbanded The Blue Flames, and had plunged boldly into 1966's self-financed *Sound Venture* LP with jazz veterans like Stan Tracey, Tubby Hayes and The Harry South Big Band. Meanwhile, Steve Winwood was in the process of forming Traffic, because he could no longer hide his real or false embarrassment whenever any of The Spencer Davis Group's early 45s shook the record player at parties.

The Tremeloes and Brian Poole were recording separately; Alan Price was notching up Top 20 entries as an ex-Animal; Denny Laine was biding his time after quitting The Moody Blues; Dave Davies had had two hits without the other Kinks; Jeff Beck was about to be sacked from an already fragmenting Yardbirds and it was Don Craine's New Downliners Sect these days. At Decca's usual Tuesday-morning board meeting, someone mentioned X-factor Van Morrison's less sweeping exit from Them, and it was decided that it would do no harm to try him out in the West Hampstead studio to see if a relaunch as either a solo attraction or as leader of a new outfit was tenable.

When Brian was in danger of going to jail, Decca insiders had kept their peace when the Stones' new manager, a cigar-chewing New York accountant named Allen Klein, had calmed press friction with, 'There is absolutely no question of bringing in a replacement.'[12] It wasn't public knowledge that Dave Mason, Traffic's soon-to-be-ex-member, was helping out on *Beggar's Banquet*, and that other guitarists were cropping up in heated discussions about a Stones US tour pencilled in for winter 1969. Among them were Mick Taylor – John Mayall's latest *wunderkind* – and Eric Clapton, now that the last note of his Cream 'supergroup' had resounded at a farewell concert at the Albert Hall in November 1968.

Whether Jones fell before he was pushed is academic because, at Cotchford Farm early in the evening on the first Sunday in June, it was one of a deputation consisting of Jagger, Richards and Charlie Watts who marshalled his words and dared the speech everyone knew had to be made. The air cleared at last, and the prevalent feeling was of release. An unsettled chapter in the respective careers of Brian and the group he'd formed had just ended, though before Charlie, Keith and Mick drove off into the dusk, not forgetting to pull over at a pre-mobile telephone kiosk somewhere to ring Bill Wyman, the possibility of Jones re-joining one day had been mentioned sham-dispassionately, even if no one present regarded it as likely.

Jones's departure from the group was worthy of an item on BBC television's *Six O'Clock News* as he wondered if it was so unreasonable for him to hold in his heart the possibility that The Rolling Stones would be recalled as just the outfit in which he'd cut his teeth before going on to bigger and better things. How could poor Brian have known that he had less than six weeks left?

13 Bringing On Back The Good Times

'Brian just didn't have it in him to be "the successful rock musician". He never held anything in reserve. He just wasted himself so quickly, and you knew he wasn't going to last, that he wasn't going to reach anywhere near middle age.'

– *Keith Richards*[1]

Barely off the stereo at Cotchford Farm was Creedence Clearwater Revival, a US act Brian found thrilling for a once-familiar rough-and-ready spontaneity fame had not obscured. Also evident onstage, their succinctness was a stimulating contrast to the tendency of other contemporary rock bands to stretch out a solitary item for up to 30 po-faced minutes.

If Californian, the outfit's spiritual home seemed to be the Deep South – as exemplified in titles like 'Born On The Bayou' and 'Mardi Gras'. Initial domestic chart strikes came with 1968's eponymous debut album and its two spin-off 45s – but after 1969's 'Proud Mary' came close to Number One, Creedence scored again, with the 12-bar 'Bad Moon Rising' topping the lists in Britain and Australia, finding favour with the heavy-rock and mainstream pop fan alike, as well as fellow musicians such as Alexis Korner, Bob Dylan – and Brian Jones.

Creedence Clearwater Revival at full blast transported Brian, however temporarily, from the country quiet as he came closer to looking to the future – or to the past. Without actually looking the part, Creedence were harking back to the energy and many of the standard chord sequences of 1950s rock 'n' roll.

With *Satanic Majesties* over-produced and too clever for the commonweal, the Stones also had dug down to a bedrock of sorts with

'Jumpin' Jack Flash', perhaps their most lasting single – and, despite Brian's statement that 'We no longer communicate musically. The Stones' music is not to my taste any more'[2] in the shallow press release about the 'amicable split',[2] he'd been proud to have played a part in both 'Jumpin' Jack Flash' and the comparably unvarnished directness of *Beggar's Banquet*, that was also helping to steer pop away from backward-running tapes, funny noises and self-conscious clutter that disguised many essentially inane artistic perceptions.

Brian was even more pleased with a promised golden handshake from the Stones of the modern equivalent of just over £1 million ($1.7 million). This would skim the surface of his debts, and hold a decision – that most noxious of human phenomena – at arm's length while he continued to take pedantic stock.

'Even though he was talking about getting a new band together and doing it all again,' speculated Keith Richards with mildly facetious hindsight, 'I don't think that's what he would have ended up doing. I think he would have gone into movie music or maybe something completely different, collecting butterflies or something.'[3]

Forming another group wasn't as obvious an option any more. 'We feel that today's scene is moving very much away from permanent groups and more towards recognition for individual musicians,' Steve Winwood had pontificated in royal plural to *Melody Maker*. 'The trend is going more in the direction of the jazz scene when musicians just jam together as they please.'[4]

In tacit endorsement in *The Rolling Stones Rock 'N' Roll Circus*, Brian had witnessed an ad hoc quintet with John Lennon, Eric Clapton, Keith Richards (on bass), Mitch Mitchell and vocalist Yoko Ono giving 'em a couple of numbers. Clapton had been in attendance, too, at a less glamorous all-day function in a Staines warehouse, where some of the ablest musical technicians of two continents merged the contents of rock and jazz. Among those caught on rarely seen film was Jack Bruce, who, with Dick Heckstall-Smith and drummer Jon Hiseman, would record a one-off jazz album the following year. The prime mover in a series of less erudite get-togethers with the likes of Al Kooper and guitarist Steve Stills – from Crosby, Stills and Nash – was Mike Bloomfield of Electric

Flag, a US 'progressive'-rock equivalent of a brass band. The edited result of one of these bashes, modestly titled *Super Session*, had been among the best-selling albums of 1968.

Even before Watts, Richards and Jagger's mission on 8 June, the clouds had parted on the gods at play at Cotchford Farm, too, after vehicles bearing illustrious callers and their instruments crunched up the gravel drive. Yet, while above having to hire backrooms of pubs and advertise in the music press now, Brian wasn't to welcome John Lennon of a disintegrating Beatles – though he and Jones spoke often on the telephone – or Noel Redding, very lately parted from The Jimi Hendrix Experience. Each had other plans, just as Brian had – albeit much vaguer ones – when he did nothing about an offer to join Humble Pie, which, following the crass 'supergroup' precedent of Cream and its Blind Faith derivative, amalgamated ex-personnel from The Small Faces, The Herd and Spooky Tooth.

In June 1969, Humble Pie booked a studio to make 'Natural Born Bugie' [*sic*], a maiden single, that, if nondescript, was at least more tangible than the musical meanderings at Cotchford Farm after Brian had picked the brains of Alexis Korner about anyone available for and interested in playing – oh, I dunno – back-to-basics, unadulterated Bricklayers' Arms blues maybe or being just like Creedence Clearwater Revival. As The Crazy World Of Arthur Brown were fresh from falling apart after a US tour, said Alexis, organist Vincent Crane and drummer Carl Palmer were at a loose end, and so was Mickey Waller, former sticksman with The Jeff Beck Group. Such was the concord with his old G Club mentor that Brian was emboldened to suggest a link-up with Alexis himself. Maybe Korner's existing New Church outfit could take him on as a guest star for an imminent trek round West Germany.

Korner changed the subject. For a start, Brian's presence onstage with any group then was likely to spark disruption beyond shouted requests for 'Ruby Tuesday', 'Jumpin' Jack Flash' *et al*. Second, despite the country air and assurances that he was off hard drugs, Jones was none too hale, physically or mentally. As well as being pale still and noticeably tubbier, he'd wake feeling groggy and out of sorts, and finish the day brimming with various medications he took compulsively to sleep, to calm his nerves, to lift his depressions and, of course, to nip the old asthma in the bud. It wasn't the firmest foundation for Brian to give the music business another whirl.

Late in June, nevertheless, he managed a journey to London to prod nerves about the non-arrival of the pay-off from the Stones. Someone from *Rolling Stone* magazine's UK office – then operating from the same premises – bumped into Brian on the stairs and asked if he fancied a cup of coffee. 'This sweating figure came in and I spent the afternoon talking to him,' recalled advertising manager Alan Marcuson, 'not knowing whether to be nice to him because he was a superstar, but he looked very ill.'[5]

Down on the farm, while she didn't quite match the ideal Brian had won and lost, Anna, the latest in a line of long-suffering live-in girlfriends, was more like a hospital orderly than passionate inamorata as she let him fulminate and bluster without reproach, and talked him through his twin paranoias: the Stones' apparent procrastination about the pledged cash, and the cowboy builders supposedly renovating the place, but behaving as if they did not know the dignity of labour.

Yet, though the psychological undergrowth was overgrown, the pathway through the woods was becoming less of an impasse as the weeks slipped by. Moreover, Brian was always capable of getting a grip on himself for the duration of visits from musicians – and for an upbeat telephone chat with Jimmy Miller: 'He said, "I'm clean. I haven't been doing any drugs. I've been down here with these young musicians, who are wonderful. We're going to do an album, and I'd like you to produce it." I said, "Brian, I haven't heard you sound this good since I've known you. I'd love to help out. When can I hear the stuff?" He said, "Why don't you give us another week. Then you can come down, and we'll do a set for you. Bring your family. Maybe stay the weekend. I've got a barbecue and a swimming pool." That was my last conversation with him.'[6]

A similar open invitation was extended to Alexis Korner, whose son Damian would remember him as 'such a nice man to be around. Brian was kind, considerate and thoughtful. He was a comforting person. If you don't have children [*sic*], you have to be a nice person in order to comfort children. Staying at the house was a problem for me because it was haunted – but he had the capacity to make a young child who was feeling frightened feel OK.'[7]

For a weekend that seemed like a fortnight, Brian's parents came to stay, too. Few say what they really mean about close relations to strangers, especially journalists. Therefore, who can guess how Mr and Mrs Jones regarded their *no-good boyo* and all the pointing fingers at the trouble there'd been over him, the child who'd influenced the lives of millions and shattered those of a few.

Had Lewis and Louise retained the knack of filling their 27-year-old son with guilt, aggravation and worthlessness – and disloyalty for even having those feelings? Had they shared his joy in May 1963, when, almost beside himself, he'd rung from a King's Road payphone about the Decca recording contract? Had they glowed with pride when 'Little Red Rooster' topped the charts? Had they put on airs after Matins, basking in his reflected glory, or were they merely resigned to the way he had chosen to make his living? Did they still deplore his personal conduct, or had they accepted him at last for what he was?

There are so many unanswerable questions about the invisible chains that shackle parent to offspring, but when it was time to go Brian squeezed his mother's hand, then changed his mind and pecked her on the cheek.

During this last month of his life, other intimates left Cotchford Farm or hung up the receiver without formal goodbyes, although wisdom after the event had some claiming that Brian seemed either strangely contemplative or overcome with rose-tinted sentiment. Yet the stirring or otherwise exploits of yore didn't impress Ian Stewart, who couldn't be persuaded to come down for a 'blow' even for old time's sake, telling Jones, 'I formed one group with you, and that was enough.'[8]

In the wee, small hours of Thursday 3 July, Ian was the first Stone to be informed that, just around midnight, an oddly lonely life had ended. That evening, Jones and his girlfriend had been drinking by the swimming pool by way of mild thanksgiving that the Stones cheque was finally on the way. With them was a fellow called Frank. He was the 44-year-old foreman of the so-called builders. Brian couldn't help liking Frank, possibly because he had a nature as recognisably unscrupulous as Brian's own. Brian couldn't help disliking Frank, either, for his uncouth manner and ineptitude. For most of the time when he'd been supervising his workforce, Frank had been conducting an extra-marital affair with a local nurse named Janet in the flatlet attached to the property in which he had billeted himself until the job was done.

Janet was present, too, at the rather boozy *soirée* by the pool. She noticed, but didn't yet say anything about, Brian washing down his usual bedtime tranquilliser with an injudicious quantity of spirits. He was also cursing that week's high pollen count that had stirred up his asthma and obliged him to resort to inhalers and antihistamine tablets throughout the previous 24 hours. Before dawn, it had invaded his bronchial tubes, and the slow pageant of sunrise became a dishevelled and feverish few hours before an unwholesome weariness overcame the running mucus, the croaking, the sniffing and the huff-puffing that were keeping Anna awake as well.

Though he'd swallowed some sort of pick-me-up to see him through the daylight hours, the small talk that evening was desultory and petering out when Brian put a full stop to it by proposing a quick dip before retiring. The news about the Stones money was resonating still and counteracting the desired effects of the drink and the pills. The floodlit water was as warm as if for a bath, and the exercise might prove enough to slip him into a blissful, dreamless and soul-satisfying sleep. However, in Janet's professional opinion, it wasn't particularly advisable, as Brian was now quite unsteady enough on dry land.

Everyone but Janet changed and swam, though. Soon, Anna and then Frank got out, dried themselves and went indoors, where Janet was picking self-consciously at one of the guitars in the music room. Sheepishly, she stopped and, suddenly aware of no sound of aquatic activity from the pool, emerged from the house to check.

Death had taken Brian Jones without effort. He'd sunk into a blue oblivion at the tiled bottom of the deep end. The heat, the alcohol, the drugs and the oncoming drowsiness had all combined to bring about his body's final rebellion after a lifetime of violation.

They dragged him out and, under Janet's panicked supervision, applied artificial respiration, cardiopulmonary resuscitation and other ministrations before the paramedics did the same. It was to no avail, and the corpse of Lewis Brian Hopkin-Jones was borne by ambulance to the morgue in the Royal Victoria Hospital in East Grinstead.

While the rest of London slumbered, the other Stones – minus Bill, who'd gone home – were told about Brian during a mixing session at Olympic Studios. Not long afterwards, an electric thrill banished sleep for obituarists, who hammered something together for the later editions of the morning newspapers and fuller stories for Sunday, such as the one entitled 'The Wicked Life Of Brian Jones' ('strangely old at twenty-five [*sic*]') in the *People*.[9] The last big show-business death had been almost exactly a year earlier, when Tony Hancock had overdosed in Australia.

Pat Andrews, Richard Hattrell and others that Brian had left behind heard about him on the radio, saw chalked headlines on newspaper stands or looked without instant comprehension at electronically transmitted images of him in electrical-goods shops.

Before twilight thickened, the black carnival was well under way. Decca, with uncalculated guile, shipped out the Stones' new single, 'Honky Tonk Woman', as scheduled, while master tapes for *Through The Past Darkly*, a 'greatest hits' compilation for release in September, were signed for at the pressing plant.

Over at the Stones office, an announcement was prepared, assuring press and public that a free show to launch the new line-up – with Mick Taylor the chosen one – on Saturday in the Cockpit, Hyde Park's natural amphitheatre, was to go ahead as planned. 'Brian would have wanted it to go on,' as Mick Jagger allowed himself to be quoted. 'We will do the concert for Brian. I hope people will understand that it is because of our love for him that we are still doing it.'[1]

Alexis Korner insisted that his New Church be among the preceding acts when the Stones presided over the largest assembly for any cultural event London had ever seen. Just before the founders of the feast commenced a two-hour set, Mick – Jagger – read excerpts from 'Adonais', Shelley's elegy for Keats, whose time on this planet was as brief as Brian's.

Pete Townshend – who recommended emulation of the Stones as a recipe for any new pop group's success – composed a private musical eulogy, 'A Normal Day For Brian, A Man Who Died Every Day'; Jimi

Hendrix dedicated a number to him during an appearance on US television; an edition of *Beat Club*, a German pop series as vital in its way as *Ready Steady Go*, was devoted to him, and Jim Morrison's 'Ode To LA While Thinking Of Brian Jones, Deceased' was published in *Disc And Music Echo*, the week after the funeral on 10 July in Cheltenham in the rain.[10]

The Stones had requested fans to stay away, but one determined bystander was admonished for standing on a headstone for an unblocked view as Alexis Korner, Ian Stewart, Charlie Watts and Bill Wyman were shepherded past hundreds – some clutching autograph books – through the lych gate and towards the main porch of St Mary's Parish Church. Hotfoot from the States, Linda Lawrence would take a pew, too, with five-year-old Julian Brian in the frilled brown jacket of his cowboy suit. No one had thought to invite Pat Andrews and Julian Mark. Carrying a bronzed metal casket topped with a floral guitar, the hearse and its retinue of limousines had crawled past spectators from upstairs office windows and roadside crowds that clotted thickest nearer the churchyard.

During the 20-minute service by the rector, Canon Hugh Evan-Hopkins began his oration for the one-time chorister by stressing how willingly he'd assented 'when Brian's parents asked, with some diffidence, whether I would allow his funeral service to take place in the parish church. Never let it be thought that the Church is less loving, less understanding, less forgiving than God himself.

'Little did Brian ever dream, when he sang in our choir here, that his musical talent would ever lead to his name hitting the headlines or that he and his colleagues – several of whom we are so glad to have with us here this afternoon – would become known far and wide because of their ability to express in word and song the feelings of literally thousands of young people.

'He was a rebel. He had little patience with authority, convention and tradition. In this, he was typical of many of his generation who have come to see in The Rolling Stones an expression of their whole attitude to life.

'Much that this ancient church has stood for for nine hundred years seems totally irrelevant to them, and yet it is not humbug to come today to offer our prayers on this tragic occasion.'[11]

As the mourners walked out for the 1.5km- (1mile-) long drive to the cemetery in Bouncer's Lane, one of several sobbing girls – three clasping single red roses – reached out to clutch the priest's hand. His other was supporting Louise Jones, who'd wept throughout the ceremony.

While he'd sent a wreath, Mick Jagger couldn't be there for the excellent reason that, during the 'Sympathy For The Devil' playout at Hyde Park, he'd been motoring across the Serpentine, bound for Ned Kelly's Australia and more lurid headlines concerning a girl and drugs. The girl was Marianne Faithfull and the drugs she took were too many Tuinals for sleeping off the jet lag, in Sydney's Chevron hotel. Lying next to an already slumbering Jagger, her thoughts were racing as she watched herself tip the capsules into her hand and send them down her neck with stark gulps of drinking chocolate. Soon, she was speaking to the late Brian until he drifted away for ever.

Marianne came round in hospital in the thick of inserted drips and tubes, with the feeling that she had stood with Brian Jones on a bridge crossing a limbo between the here and the hereafter.

Epilogue
Stone Dead

'"Hey! You! Get off of my cloud!" That's what Rolling Stone
Brian Jones has told dead fans who've been squatting in the
grounds of his exclusive $500,000 [£300,000] Heaven mansion.'
 – 'Heavens Above: afterlife gossip with the late Fanny Batter'[1]

The coroner concluded that it was 'death by misadventure'. While the
jigsaw puzzle of the final years of the lost life revealed a musician
demoralised and drug-addled, Brian Jones had not been on the brink of
a self-administered end. 'Carl Palmer and I had an appointment to see
him the day after he was found in his swimming pool,' testified Vincent
Crane, 'so I'm convinced that he didn't commit suicide.'[2]

Extravagant theories about circumstances more sinister by those who
weren't there were going the rounds even as pressured journalists assigned
to the story were still under the editorial lash, and estate agents hadn't
stopped wondering who was doing the probate assessment. Morbid
inquisitiveness about Brian's drowning continues to this day, but if foul
play took place the 'chief suspect' – Frank the philandering cowboy
builder – is gone too; nobody else involved has total recall and, to quote
the title of a 1966 Kinks' album track, the world keeps going round. The
facts will never be known. Let's get on with our lives like the Stones did
after the Hyde Park memorial concert.

With Mick Taylor firmly in harness, the group went back on the road
again, beginning with a US barnstormer as the decade turned. Rather
than 30 closing minutes on the scream circuit, they were now delivering
three-hour spectaculars where matches would be lit and held up *en masse*
in trendy approval. On the minus side, discomforted snarls had replaced

1967's peace and love as everyone with the same-priced tickets pushed towards the protecting cordon of hired security. Onstage silences and pianissimos were undermined by a barrage of whistling, stamping and, worst of all, bellowed demands for the good old good ones.

'Paint It Black' was dropped from the set for decades. When restored, the sitar part was approximated on electric guitar. 'Lady Jane', 'Back Street Girl' and like numbers freighted with Brian's greater subtleties were deemed unworkable for audiences, many tens of thousands strong, that had bought tickets for a tribal gathering rather than a musical recital.

Like the inverse of a fisherman's tall tale, Jones's irretractable contributions on disc were minimalised, too, by certain Stones down the days to such a degree that Pat Andrews was driven to protest that 'Mick and Keith believed that because they were closer to London, they knew it all – and then this guy from the provinces arrives. He's a better musician with more savvy than them, and shows them what's what. The greatest injustice to Brian is that the Stones, apart from Bill, have never really thanked him, because without him they'd have never been in the position they're in now. They seem to want to forget him.'

Pat ascribed it to jealousy, but, when endeavouring to make a BBC2 documentary about Brian on the tenth anniversary of his death, Jonathan Meades discovered 'a general feeling of embarrassment about Jones among the people in the Stones' court, a sort of collective guilt about the way he had been treated. It was all too clearly a dog-eats-dog sort of milieu.'

Yet one of Brian's progeny gained well-paid behind-the-scenes employment within the Stones organisation, and Mick Jagger sent flowers when The Brian Jones Fan Club convened at the graveside on 3 July 1996.

To a more pragmatic end, the highlight of 1989's *Steel Wheels* was 'Continental Drift', a 'twinning' of the Stones and The Master Musicians Of Joujouka to infuse it with an essential ingredient of North African mysticism. 'Brian turned us onto it years ago,' admitted Mick Jagger, 'and I wanted to try something in the same vein myself. To be honest, I thought it would end up on one of my solo records. I never thought the Stones would buy it, but Keith was well into it. We worked something out on a keyboard first, and then went to Morocco to record the real thing. In a way, it's a continuation of the 'Paint It Black'-*Satanic Majesties* thing, but heading off a bit more into Brian's territory. It's the same group Brian recorded more than twenty years ago.'[3]

'It is as though the spirit of Brian Jones, the real soul of The Rolling Stones, has entered into the music,' agreed a glowing *NME* appraisal. 'It is a both moving and honest tribute to yet another master musician.'[3]

A more palpable acknowledgement was US guitar manufacturers Korg introducing reproductions of Brian's Vox Teardrop Mk VI, renamed the Mk III BJ in his honour, in 1998.

Collectors of Stones-associated memorabilia will find more intrinsic value in 1986's 'Godstar', a vinyl salute to Jones that, at Number 67 in the UK charts, was the closest Psychic TV and the Angels Of Light, a multimedia ensemble risen from the confrontational ashes of 'industrial' music pioneers Throbbing Gristle, came to a *Top Of The Pops* appearance.

Psychic TV's mainstay, Neil 'Genesis P Orridge' Megson[4], also made contact with Pat Andrews in the early 1960s after a Requiem Mass for Brian at St Philip and St Steven's Church in Up Hatherley, a Cheltenham suburb. The service, conceived by Father John Heidt, had been held annually for almost a decade, but was to cease on Heidt's return to his native North Amercia in 1993. However, a few devotees decided to form a fan club to ensure, at least from their perspective, Brian's spirit would live on, choosing *The Spirit* as the name of the associated fanzine.[5]

Among recent activites has been a campaign for a street on a new housing estate in Cheltenham to be named Brian Jones Close. Despite support from local MP Nigel Jones this has, reportedly, met opposition from residents and potential buyers. There has also been talk of a statue along the Promenade.

Moreover, in July 1994, on the 25th anniversary of Brian's passing, around 300 people – some from as far away as Japan and California – paid £25 ($42) per head to enter Cheltenham racecourse for 12 hours of Noel Redding, Dick Heckstall-Smith, The Downliners Sect, Brian Knight and other artists once associated with the departed.

Now in their 80s, Lewis and Louise Jones continued to pray for the soul of their son in St Mary's. Brian's sister Barbara, a physiotherapist, never left Cheltenham either – at least, not until she retired.

Richard Hattrell, however, returned to the capital, where he rose to the rank of head bartender at the plush Tower Thistle Hotel, next to Tower Bridge. 'I created a cocktail for Prince Charles's engagement,' said Richard with quiet pride, 'and got on nationwide TV after I received a letter from Buckingham Palace, thanking me.' In the 1990s, he began running Red Hot Jazz Management, specialising in providing British and North American acts mostly for venues *sur le continent*.

He remains friends with Pat Andrews, who lives in the same part of south London. Emerging from the *Man Alive* ravine, she'd found vocational contentment working with disabled children, and as a superintendent of a charity that provided inner-city youngsters with regular activity holidays. In the 1970s, she became a schoolteacher. Other members of staff might have deduced from the odd secret smile and what was left unsaid that Miss Andrews had had an intriguing previous existence.

This reared up with unprecedented abundance when, on behalf of the fan club, she reviewed a performance by The Railing Stains, a tribute band that paid specific homage to Brian. After the show, one thing led to another, and Pat found herself before a studio microphone, singing backing vocals on the group's recording of 'Ruby Tuesday'. She also ventured onto the boards – notably when the Stains saw in the new millennium at Brighton Pavilion before the biggest crowd of their career, and at Cotchford Farm, for the 21st birthday party of the daughter of the house.

Extensive repairs had been made to the swimming pool, and the old loose tiles had been sold as souvenirs via the Internet.

Appendix

By Trevor Hobley, The Brian Jones Fan Club

What really happened to the founding member of The Rolling Stones late into the evening of 2 July 1969? Numerous theories abound: accident, suicide, murder – who knows? Numerous books, newspaper and magazine articles have been dedicated to that evening's events and now, at the time of going to press, a film is in production purporting to tell the truth about that fateful night. Had Brian survived, he would now be approaching 'retirement', but he did not get the chance to grow old with his fellow Stones. Instead, he remains forever young, frozen in time as the musical icon of the '60s, up there in the pantheon of rock legends but now ten feet under in a Cheltenham graveyard. That Brian departed this world confused and alone, no longer a member of the group he founded, is surely one of the most tragic stories in the history of popular music.

In the latter part of this edition, Alan Clayson talks of the enthusiastic fans who go to great lengths to keep Brian's memory alive. Individuals closely associated with The Brian Jones Fan Club have, for almost a decade, with few resources except sheer determination, researched the circumstances surrounding Brian's death. There's an old saying that once you open a can of worms you need a bigger can to put them back into, and such is the case with Brian's death. According to Brian's supporters, the public in general are oblivious to the tale of betrayal, corruption, thuggery and cover-up surrounding his 'death by misadventure' and until the real facts are brought out into the public domain the Establishment will continue to disregard the damning evidence that points to murder. Ignorance is bliss, but it is this complacency which allows the guilty ones to hide behind a cloak of anonymity, and the more evidence that surfaces gives credence to the words of Brian's friend Ronny Money: 'there was dirty work at Cotchford that night'.

To trace the origins of Brian's demise, let's rewind to the mid-'60s when Britain was a nation regarded as the epitome of self-restraint and stiff upper lip, dominated by stuffy middle-class values. The pressure on the Stones during this period was intense and after the '67 drug bust, the subsequent trial merely enhanced Mick and Keith's reputations as social outlaws; but for Brian it marked the beginning of his descent into a living hell – the '60s were swinging away from him.

There were two detectives in the Chelsea Drug Squad who made Brian's life such a misery. One was Detective Sergeant Norman Pilcher (lampooned by John Lennon in 'I Am The Walrus' with his lyrics 'semolina pilchards, crawling up the Eiffel Tower'), who was extradited from Australia to face charges of corruption and was thrown out of the police force in 1973. The second, Detective Sergeant Robin Constable, who was instrumental in busting Mick Jagger and Marianne Faithfull in 1969, was similarly expelled from the force.

Hospitalised twice during 1967 suffering from nervous exhaustion, Brian was fading fast; a psychiatrist's report revealed that 'he has an IQ of 133, but is losing his grip on reality. He vacillates between a passive, dependent child with a confused image of an adult on one hand and an idol of pop culture on the other'.

After Brian moved out of his Courtfield Road apartment, following the first drug bust in May 1967, he led a rootless existence, moving between various hotels, flats and nursing homes, but these attempts to stay one step ahead of his tormentors proved futile. Matters came to a head in May 1968, when Brian was busted for possession of cannabis for the second time in what was a blatant set-up. (Fleet Street hacks had even been tipped off in advance to get ready to run with a story of a Rolling Stones drug bust.) Even fellow guitarist Keith Richards was sympathetic: 'They really roughed him up, they went for him like when hound dogs smell blood. There's one that'll break if we keep it up and they busted him and busted him'.

The Stones, meanwhile, had a hard but inevitable decision to make. With their finances in disarray it was essential to tour again, especially with two albums' worth of new material ready for an eager audience. But Brian was a problem, and so it was in early June 1969 that Keith, Mick and Charlie travelled down to Cotchford to tell him that he was no longer a Rolling Stone. Many years later Charlie Watts would describe Brian's sacking as the worst thing he'd ever had to do. The fragile friendships from those early days of struggle in the pubs and clubs of London had counted for nothing – Brian had lost his band to Mick, his girlfriend to Keith and on the night of 2–3 July 1969, he would lose his life.

The two detectives who investigated Brian's death were Detective Chief Inspector Marshall and Detective Sergeant Hunter. Robert Marshall, a proud man with an exemplary track record, was aware that there was a 'considerable amount of prestige to be gained by solving the death of a celebrity' and Mick Martin, Brian's gardener, remembered the senior detective confiding to him that he was convinced there was a charge of at least manslaughter to be brought against one individual. However, somewhere down the line the police lost their appetite for the case. In no way can Marshall and Hunter be criticised because it is clear that they had their hands tied on this one. After Sussex CID referred the case to the Director of Public Prosecutions, the Home Office launched their own investigation and it was at this stage that a higher authority decided to cover up the whole affair.

If you think it sounds fanciful, then consider this: in the eyes of the Establishment, Brian's death was the logical conclusion to a lifestyle which had spiralled out of control, and to them one dead ex-Rolling Stone was no big deal. Would the authorities have wanted to make a martyr out of someone they regarded with contempt, whose profligate lifestyle represented the new hedonism the older generation abhorred? And would the legal authorities have wanted to spend thousands of pounds of taxpayers' money on a high-profile trial when they had a perfect opportunity to send out a warning to the nation's youth that Brian Jones exemplified a decadent lifestyle which had fittingly resulted in his death?

When East Sussex Coroner Angus Somerville delivered his verdict of 'death by misadventure, drowning whilst under the influence of alcohol and drugs', sure enough, a headline-grabbing stitch-up was lying in wait, and the 'Gotcha!' gutter press had a field day with all their lurid revelations. But did they know that vital pieces of information were disregarded and glossed over at the hastily-convened inquest held at East Grinstead on 7 July, only five days after Brian's death? Was this enough time to gather all the facts and necessary evidence? The authorities it seems, wanted the whole case swept under the carpet. Nobody yet, is forthcoming with any answers – but time will tell...

Notes

In addition to my own correspondence and interviews, I have used the following sources, which I would like to credit:

Prologue: Foundation Stone

1   *Lennon Remembers* ed. J Wenner (Penguin, 1972)

Chapter 1: Along Came Jones

1   *Blues In Britain* by B Brunning (Blandford, 1995)

2   *NME*, 27 November 1964

3   *Faithfull* by M Faithfull and D Dalton (Michael Joseph, 1994)

4   *Folk And Rock* (French journal, summer 1987)

Chapter 2: Someone Else's Baby

1   *New Orleans Joys* by Chris Barber's New Orleans Jazz Band (Decca LF 1198, 10in, 1954)

2   *Skiffle* by B Bird (Robert Hale, 1958)

3   *Chris Barber In Concert Volume Three* (Pye NJL 17, 1958)

4   To Robin Brooks (*Gloucestershire Echo*)

5   Graham Ride, sometime flatmate of Brian Jones, is the author of *Foundation Stone* (Broad Brush, 2001), a memoir of his association with the former Rolling Stone and the interrelated jazz and blues scene in Cheltenham.

6   *A Guide To Popular Music* by P Gammond and P Clayton (Phoenix House, 1960)

7   Who was, incidentally, to take up residency in Halifax.

8   Particularly as there was a US Ramrods, who'd reach the British Top 10 in 1961 with an arrangement of '(Ghost) Riders In The Sky'.

9   *Days In The Life: Voices From The English Underground 1961–1971* ed. J Green (Heinemann, 1988)

10 'The Blood Donor' (first broadcast on 23 June 1961)

11 *Radio Times*, 14 July 1956

12 *Hamburg: The Cradle Of British Rock* by A Clayson (Sanctuary, 1997)

13 *Scouting For Boys* by Lord Baden-Powell (C Arthur Pearson, 1949)

14 A pre-1970 euphemism for fondling ('desert sickness' = wandering palms).

15 *Sunday Mirror*, 8 January 1969

16 This grim chapter of Irish history was the subject of *The Magdalen Sisters*, an acclaimed 2002 film.

17 Valerie was to marry Graham Ride.

Chapter 3: Beatnik Fly

1 *Melody Maker*, 23 November 1969

2 *Blues Fell This Morning* by P Oliver (Cassell, 1960)

3 To Robin Brooks

4 A beat group from Hull, led by the late Mick Ronson. In the 1970s, he and other Rats were to be absorbed into David Bowie's backing group, The Spiders From Mars.

5 *Jimi Hendrix* by B Mann (Orion, 1994)

6 *Skiffle* by B Bird (Robert Hale, 1958)

7 *Ken Colyer's Jazzmen* (Tempo EXA 26, 1953)

8 My friend Kevin defaced a school atlas, trying to figure exactly how 'it winds from Chicago to LA' – though the only version I've ever heard on which you could make out all the words was by Bing Crosby and The Andrews Sisters.

9 *Manchester Evening News*, 27 October 1957

Chapter 4: Halfway To Paradise

1 *Days In The Life: Voices From The English Underground 1961–1971* ed. J. Green (Heinemann, 1988)

2 *Talk To Me Baby: The Story Of The Blues Band* by R Bainton (Firebird, 1994)

3 *Folk Roots*, 19 May 1989

4 Ian Stewart quoted in *Alexis Korner: The Biography* by H Shapiro (Bloomsbury, 1996)

5 *Melody Maker*, 11 March 1962

Chapter 5: Bachelor Boy

1 *Top Twenty* ed. P Buckle (Purnell, 1966)

2 Actually a studio recording, as *Jimmy Reed At Carnegie Hall* had been.

3   *Beat Merchants* by A Clayson (Blandford, 1995)

4   *Blues In Britain* by B Brunning (Blandford, 1995)

5   They were managed by a Mr Turner. Mick Jagger was to play a character called Turner in the 1970 movie *Performance*. Weird, eh?

6   *Hampstead And Highgate Express*, 30 October 1964

7   *New Musical Express Encyclopaedia Of Rock* ed. N Logan and B Woffinden (Salamander, 1976)

8   *The Rolling Stones: Best Of Guitar Player* ed. J Obrecht (Miller Freeman, 1995)

9   *Brian Jones: Rock & Roll Never Forgets* (US radio documentary, 1984)

10   *Record Collector*, April 2001

11   *Jazz News*, 21 November 1962

12   *X-Ray* by R Davies (Viking 1994)

13   *London Live* by Tony Bacon (Balafon, 1999)

Chapter 6: Go Away Little Girl

1   *Yardbirds World* ed. R Mackay and M Ober (privately published, 1989)

2   *Yardbirds World* ed. R Mackay and M Ober (privately published, 1989). The headache-inducing Shake was also known as the Root, because participants remained rooted to the spot and shook their heads to the beat.

3   After saxophonist Watson's violent death during a fracas at the Flamingo on a subsequent night, singing organist Georgie Fame took over as leader of The Blue Flames

4   *Teenbeat Annual 1968* (World Distributors, 1967)

5   *Keith Richards In His Own Words* ed. M St Michael (Omnibus, 1994)

6   *Stoned: A Memoir Of London In The 1960s* by A Oldham (St Martin's Press, 2000)

7   *Q*, May 1995

8   *Back In The High Life* by A Clayson (Sidgwick and Jackson, 1988)

Chapter 7: Devil In Disguise

1   *Record Collector*, July 1989

2   *Record Mirror*, 8 June 1963

3   To Robin Brooks

4   *Record Collector*, July 1995

5   *NME*, 12 March 1964

6   *NME*, 15 November 1963. The 'mail bags' reference is to do with 1963's Great Train Robbery, in which a gang of thugs, since romanticised as 20th-century highwaymen, made off with swag worth more than £2 million ($3 million).

7   *NME*, 27 November 1964

8   Quoted in sleeve notes to *Count On Me* by Julie Grant (RPM 133, 1994)

9   *Beat Merchants* by A Clayson (Blandford, 1995)

10 *NME*, 23 August 1963

11 *Daily Sketch*, 27 May 1964

12 *Keith Richards In His Own Words* ed. M St Michael (Omnibus, 1994)

13 Brian's choice as the follow-up to 'Come On' had been 'Fortune Teller', a number that was common property of scores of beat groups.

14 *Rolling Stones Monthly*, May 1965

15 *And The Beat Still Goes On*, February 2003

16 They were succeeded by The Ramblers, 'the great new pop music group', according to the packet. A signed photograph of The Ramblers was sent to every entrant in a Rice Krispies competition to win an electric guitar.

17 Part of the deal was that the firm – Jennings of Dartford, Kent – would provide the Stones with amplifiers. Vox also manufactured guitars. Brian Jones played one of their 1961 two pick-up Teardrop Mk VIs, though later he was to use a sunburst Gibson Firebird VII (of off-kilter oblong shape) and, for bottleneck, a Melobar, invented in 1967 to enable electric slide players to stand up.

18 Sleeve notes by A Clayson to *The Definitive Downliners Sect: Singles A's & B's* (See For Miles SEECD 398, 1994).

19 *Record Mirror*, 7 January 1964

20 Quoted in *Swinging Sheffield* by A Clayson (Sheffield Museum, 1993)

21 *Rock's Wild Things: The Troggs Files* by A Clayson and J Ryan (Helter Skelter, 2000)

22 *Rock 'N' Reel No.* 35, winter 2001

23 *The Yardbirds* by A Clayson (Backbeat, 2002)

24 *Call Up The Groups!* by A Clayson (Blandford, 1983)

Chapter 8: Don't Talk To Him

1   *Blues In Britain* by B Brunning (Blandford, 1995)

2   'Phelge' was after Jones, Richards and Jagger's former flatmate, and 'Nanker' was Brian's word for a face he used to pull to cheer up Keith during the Edith Grove winter.

3   *Record Collector*, April 2001

4   *Melody Maker*, 23 November 1969

5   *Rock And Folk*, May 1984

6   *Keith Richards In His Own Words* ed. M St Michael (Omnibus, 1994)

7   *The Story Of The Shadows* by M Read (Elm Tree, 1983)

8   In 1969, Jet (then a West Country bus conductor) was to marry his second wife at the registry office in Cheltenham of all places.

9   *Ugly Things*, No.19, summer 2001

10 *NME*, 24 May 1964

11 *Disc*, 24 November 1962

12 *Beatboom!* by D McAleer (Hamlyn, 1994)

13 *NME*, 17 July 1964

14 *Gloucestershire Echo: The Sixties*, souvenir guide, August 1968

15 Bill Wyman's stage announcement at 2002's Cheltenham Jazz Festival.

16 *The Rolling Stones As It Happened: The Classic Interviews* (Chrome Dreams CIS 2002/1, 2001)

17 As he had been already for five dates in September 1963, owing to illness

18 *Midland Beat*, No.11, August 1964

19 *Mersey Beat*, 9 April 1964

Chapter 9: Golden Lights

1   *Q*, July 1990

2   *NME*, 17 July 1964

3   *Record Collector*, July 1989

4   *Record Collector*, April 2001

5   *NME*, August 1965 (precise date obscured)

Chapter 10: It's Not Unusual

1   Donovan was to marry Linda Lawrence at Windsor Registry Office on 2 October 1970. His million-selling 'Sunshine Superman' was, purportedly, dedicated to Linda.

2   To Spencer Leigh

3   *NME*, 26 March 1965

4   *Kink* by D Davies (Boxtree, 1996)

5   *Blues In Britain* by B Brunning (Blandford, 1995)

6   *Rolling Stones '76* ed. M Farren (Cumbergrove, 1976)

7   It was covered immediately in quasi-easy-listening fashion by The Deep Six, a San Diego-based sextet through whose ranks passed David Gates of Bread and Glen Campbell. In 2002, the Stones' 'Paint It Black' was at No.8 in the Performing Rights Society's chart of the most popular songs played on UK jukeboxes.

8   *Record Collector*, July 1989

9   *Zigzag* (date obscured)

10 *Keith Richards In His Own Words* ed. M St Michael (Omnibus, 1994)

11 *Faithfull* by M Faithfull and D Dalton (Penguin, 1995)

12 *Faithfull* by M Faithfull and D Dalton (Penguin, 1995). In parenthesis, 'Ruby Tuesday' was covered – as 'Fille Sauvage' – in France by Richard Anthony, accompanied by The Roulettes, Adam Faith's former backing group.

13 Owned by the husband of Jane Rainey, daughter of Lord Harlech. This lent substance to a *Daily Express* gossip columnist assurance to readers that, 'There's no harm these days in knowing a Rolling Stone. Some of their best friends, in fact, are fledglings from the upper classes', quoted in *Beat Merchants* by A Clayson (Blandford, 1995).

14 *Alexis Korner* by H Shapiro (Bloomsbury, 1996)

15 *NME*, 4 February 1967

16 *Daily Mail*, 18 July 1990

Chapter 11: Silence Is Golden

1   *Daily Mail*, 18 July 1990

2   *Turn Off Your Mind* by G Valentine Lachman (Sidgwick and Jackson, 2001)

3   *Faithfull* by M Faithfull and D Dalton (Penguin, 1995)

4   *The John Lennon Encyclopaedia* by B Harry (Virgin, 2000)

5   *Paul McCartney; Many Years From Now* by B Miles (Vintage, 1998)

6   *NME*, 21 October 1966

7   *Ugly Things*, No.18, summer 2000

8   *Keith Richards In His Own Words* ed. M St Michael (Omnibus, 1994)

9   *NME*, 4 February 1967

10 *The Yardbirds* by A Clayson (Backbeat, 2002)

11 *Guardian*, 30 August 1990

12 *Don't Let Me Be Misunderstood* by E Burdon and J Marshall Craig (Thundermouth, 2001)

13 *Rhino's Psychedelic Trip* by A Bisbort and P Puterbaugh (Miller Freeman, 2000)

14 Brian is mentioned also in the lyrics of 'Love On An Eleven-Year-Old Level' by The GTOs on their only album, 1970's *Permanent Damage*.

15 *Q*, June 1990

Chapter 12: Little Arrows

1   *Daily Mail*, 18 July 1990

2   On 12 May 1968, nine days after what turned out to be Brian's last ever stage performance – with the Stones at another *NME* Poll Winners Concert.

3   *Keith Richards In His Own Words* ed. M St Michael (Omnibus, 1994)

4   Years later, Pilcher of the Yard would be jailed for corrupting the course of justice.

5   *Record Collector*, November 1993

6   *Q*, October 1989

7   *Record Collector*, April 2001

8   Though its working title was 'One Plus One'.

9   *Record Collector*, July 1989

10   Sleeve notes of *Brian Jones Presents The Pipes Of Pan At Joujouka* (Rolling Stones COC 49100, 1971).

11   Trivia freaks might like to know that Roger Winslet, father of Hollywood film actor Kate, was one of the team of builders.

12   *NME*, 14 November 1967

Chapter 13: Bringing On back The Good Times

1   *Rolling Stones '76* ed. M Farren (Cumbergrove, 1976)

2   *Record Collector*, April 2001. In the magazine *Private Eye*, the press release had been satirised thus with Brian as 'Enoch Hogg' and The Rolling Stones as 'The Turds': '"People have been putting it about that I am nothing but an extremely unpleasant, untalented big-head who is stoned out of his mind day and night,"drooled Hogg, "but to my way of thinking, that is frankly wrong. It is simply a matter of basic difference between me and Spiggy Topes [Mick Jagger or Keith Richards] in our concept of the future of the group's musical policy. Me and the group are still mates, and we have a lot in common like our birds and that. Anyway, The Turds have been making a bad scene recently, and it is time we found a new gimmick to get back in the headlines like splitting up"' – *Private Pop Eye: The Life And Times Of Spiggy Topes* (Pressdram, 1969)

3   *Keith Richards In His Own Words* ed. M St Michael (Omnibus, 1994)

4   *Melody Maker*, 7 December 1968

5   *Days In The Life: Voices From The English Underground 1961–1971* ed. J Green (Heinemann, 1988)

6   *Record Collector*, November 1993

7   *Alexis Korner* by H Shapiro (Bloomsbury, 1996)

8   Translation from *Con Le Mie Lacrime* (Italian fanzine, November 1986)

9   *People*, 6 July 1969

10   *Disc And Music Echo*, 18 July 1969. Morrison described Brian Jones's drowning as a 'chlorine dream'. Collators of macabre coincidences will be intrigued by the information that Morrison sustained a fatal heart attack in a bath on 3 July 1971. Notice how both he and Jones died in water on the same day of the year? Weird, eh?

11   *Gloucestershire Echo*, 11 July 1969

Epilogue: Stone Dead

1   *Viz On The Bone* ed. C Donald (John Brown, 1998)

2   *Record Collector*, July 1989

3   *NME*, 2 September 1989. I must add the raw information that handbills distributed outside London's Royal Festival Hall in May 1999 claimed that The Master Musicians Of Joujouka appearing there that month – and, by implication, on 'Continental Drift' – were not the genuine article.

4   Megson also attempted to raise cash for a Brian Jones film, also to be titled 'Godstar', long before *The Wicked World Of Brian Jones*. Psychic TV headlined at a Royal Festival Hall show in 1999, also featuring The Master Musicians Of Joujouka (see note 3 above), as well as Thee Headcoats, the late Quentin Crisp and the original line-up of ? And The Mysterions.

5   The name of the fanzine has been changed since, from *The Spirit* to *Aftermath*. The fan club's website address is www.brianjonesfanclub.com

Index